KISSING
USA

KISSING USA

THE STORY
BEHIND THE STORY OF
THE LEGENDARY KISSING SHOW

WILLIAM CANE

CLEiS
PRESS

Published in the United States by Cleis Press, an imprint of Start Midnight, LLC, 101 Hudson Street, Thirty-Seventh Floor, Suite 3705, Jersey City, NJ 07302.

Printed in the United States
Cover design: Allyson Fields
Cover photograph: iStock
Text design: Frank Wiedemann
First Edition
10 9 8 7 6 5 4 3 2 1

Trade paper ISBN: 978-1-62778-289-0
E-book ISBN: 978-1-62778- 502-0

Library of Congress Cataloging-in-Publication Data is available on file.

For A. H.

CONTENTS

PREFACE

I WROTE *THE ART OF KISSING* TO TRY TO improve my sex life, but it didn't work. Instead, it raised women's expectations beyond what any man could meet.

Still, it has been a wild ride, and an enjoyable one too, especially because my book *The Art of Kissing* led to my being invited to speak at more than four hundred colleges and universities across North America. At each of these schools I would ask the host to provide student volunteers to demonstrate the kisses from my book. I would show up two hours before the performance and rehearse four student couples backstage. Then we would go out and give the audience the show of their life, with the volunteers demonstrating thirty different romantic kisses onstage. There has never been anything like it.

And yet a full account of how the kissing show was born—and developed into one of the most popular live shows on the college lecture circuit—has never been told until now. When I reflect back on the many people who must have wondered about the genesis of this madcap little adventure, I feel something bordering on a moral obligation to satisfy their curiosity and explain exactly how and why it all got started. Along the way, you're going to pick up useful pointers about plenty of different kisses, including the upside-down kiss, the vacuum kiss, the Trobriand Islands kiss, and of course the french kiss. For many years I hesitated to tell this story since, when you get right down to it, the sequence of events reveals how foolish I was and how many mistakes I made. But literally hundreds of print, radio, and television reporters have badgered me with questions about why I wrote the book and created the show, and readers have posed the same questions countless times. I feel it's only fair to finally stop holding back the truth.

And so, let the curtain rise!

Here for the first time ever is the full story of the origin of the legendary kissing show. . . . We begin in medias res with one of the biggest mistakes I ever made. It happened one night in Alabama, when I neglected to keep in mind that I was speaking in a conservative part of the country. I have a feeling you're going to get a kick out of this.

William Cane
New York, 2019

THE UNIVERSITY OF ALABAMA

SHORTLY AFTER SEVEN P.M. I WALKED ONTO the gymnasium stage at the University of Alabama and was greeted by a thousand cheering students. I had been introduced as the author of *The Art of Kissing*. Onstage with me were eight volunteer couples who were neatly dressed and sitting facing the audience. In a few minutes they would turn toward each other and begin kissing. The crowd knew this was going to happen, but they could hardly believe it.

The audience had entered the gym fully aware that they were about to see a kissing demonstration, yet they didn't know exactly what to expect. They were filled with anticipation; in fact, their imaginations were working overtime.

I stood smiling at them, waiting for them to quiet down so that I could begin. Every seat was filled, but people were still pouring into the room. Droves of sorority girls dressed to the nines packed the house, and the hubbub of the crowd made it impossible to concentrate. They were electrified with excitement, and I hadn't even said a word yet. It looked to me like this was shaping up to be the best show of my career. By this time I had directed literally hundreds of performances of the kissing show at colleges and universities across North America. My lecture agents had informed me that the show's popularity was growing exponentially because after each performance students would rave about it to friends at other schools: "You *have* to see this!" Word of mouth travels fast with college students, and as a result I was doing back-to-back shows, sometimes two performances at different colleges on the same day.

I gazed out at the sea of faces, amazed that 90 percent of them were girls. The show almost always drew more girls than boys, but at other campuses the composition had never been this skewed. What could have caused the preponderance of young women at this school? The only thing that came to mind was something that the president of the entertainment committee had said to me before the show. A businesslike young black man wearing a white shirt, conservative tie, and polished shoes, he had mentioned that sororities were coming to the event. Colleges are intimate communities where news often circulates with the rapidity of wildfire. The idea of going to the kissing show had apparently spread from sorority house to sorority house, and by seven o'clock every girl on that campus knew about the event: it was the kind of thing where if you didn't attend, you would be considered unfashionable and out of touch. More amazing is that all this happened in 1999, before the widespread use of social media and cell phones. This was the kind of herd mentality—in perhaps the best sense of the term—that attracted young people to this show like flies to honey. There were so many girls in the room that it seemed to have mesmerized the scattering of boys sitting in the audience.

I had no idea that this auspicious beginning was destined to turn into one of the worst nightmares of my career. How could I have known? After all, everyone seemed to be smiling and having a good time. The only strange thing about the event was the curious fact that most of the girls entering the gym were not looking at the stage or at me; instead, they were focusing on their friends and girls in the other sororities. But why? What was really going on within that standing-room-only crowd?

Only in retrospect did I realize that the sorority sisters *had* to be there; that evening, it was the place to be. And more than that, they wanted to be seen attending the event, as if their presence would serve as proof positive that they had fulfilled their social obligations.

I began to deliver my introduction: I told a few jokes and explained that by the end of the hour they would learn so many new kisses and techniques that they would enjoy a lifetime advantage over any kissing partner. As expected, the audience reacted with laughter and good-natured elbowing of friends. Some of the young women even looked up from their sorority sisters at the stage. Things were starting to click. Having directed the show hundreds of times, I could sense from their reaction to each gag exactly how closely the audience was following me. I could even predict with a fair degree of accuracy how they would react to the next bit of my material— the quotations from my book, and after that the various kissing demonstrations.

Naturally, I had rehearsed my demonstrators before- hand—eight couples that the school had rounded up in advance. We had met an hour prior to curtain time in the offices of the Campus Activities Board, where these volunteers practiced the kisses with their partners. Gently guiding them, I brought out the best they had to offer, but I also made sure that they didn't expend all their energy in the rehearsal, since it was important that they save their best romantic moves for the performance.

As was my custom, I walked into the house during the show and, carrying a battery-powered microphone, directed the action from the floor. But so many people had packed into the gym that I found it impossible to reach the rear of the room like I usually did: I had to be content with walking back and forth in front of the stage. Girls were sitting on the floor, standing against the walls, and even crammed two to a chair. I was stepping over legs and trying not to bump into them. I realized I had to get back up on the stage because there were just too many people in the room.

And here is where I made my big mistake. I was in the Deep South, a part of Alabama that's smack-dab in the middle of the Bible Belt. It had not crossed my mind that the young man who had brought me to this event, the president of the entertainment committee, was extremely conservative. He had impressed me because unlike most college students he had been wearing a suit. But it occurred to me later that he had been more serious than most students and seemed to personify a sober-minded maturity unlike anything I had ever encountered on a college campus. Unfortunately, when I launched into the underwater kiss, I had no idea that I was asking for trouble.

"Intimate kissing always involves the tongue," I began. "And this means saliva. Now, I want our volunteers to show you that a wet kiss is nothing to be afraid of. We're going to demonstrate the wettest kiss of all—an underwater kiss. So I'd like you to imagine that these girls are in the shower, lathering themselves up."

At this point the male volunteers took a giant step backward to showcase their partners, who had been rehearsed to act like they were in the shower. The girls started lathering their bodies, and I continued narrating.

"Her boyfriend comes into the bathroom, but he can't *see anything* through that *steamed-up* shower door. . . ."

The boys mimed trying to peer through the glass door.

"So he rubs a spot off the door where *he wants to see*."

The boys now rubbed a spot off the shower door so that they could peek inside. One cleared an area near his partner's backside, another near his partner's torso, and wherever they wiped those shower doors they exposed body parts that they wished to view. Imagining the nudity that the boys were revealing, the audience howled with delight. My volunteers were completely clothed, but college students have active imaginations. This was a suggestive moment in the show, but hardly an X-rated one.

Suddenly, down on the floor, someone began to yell. Over the din of the crowd I couldn't understand what he was saying, so I continued directing the skit. But this offstage voice grew louder and more strident, and I eventually recognized it as coming from the president of the entertainment committee—

"Stop right now! Stop this show!"

At first I didn't believe what I was hearing, and I ignored him. But he continued screaming at me. He didn't have a microphone, but I could hear him yelling, *"Stop! This is going too far! The show is over!"*

Finally it penetrated my slow-witted brain that this fellow seriously wanted me to stop the show. True, he was the one who booked me to speak at this school, but there were fifteen hundred students in the audience now and I had no intention of stopping the performance. Most of the crowd couldn't hear him—they could only hear me because I had the microphone—so I kept going and ignored the president of the entertainment committee.

I made it through the rest of the performance without incident . . . but when it was over, this profoundly upset young man marched up to me and announced, "You're *never* coming back to the University of Alabama."

And I never did.

Was there a lesson to be learned here? Yes, and I learned it the hard way. The lesson was simple: know your audience. I grew up and was educated in the Northeast, which is rather liberal, and the schools where I directed my first few shows all accepted the zany skits I incorporated into the act. In New York, Connecticut, Massachusetts, and Rhode Island no one ever complained about the shower kiss—on the contrary, they loved it and laughed at its risqué silliness.

But when you board an airplane, you can quickly find yourself in an area of the country where the mind-set of an audience is radically different from what you're accustomed to, and this is precisely what happened the first time I visited Alabama.

From that day forward I invited the president of the entertainment committee into the rehearsal room with us. This way the student in charge could preview the skits, and if any of them seemed objectionable, I could be instructed to leave them out of the show. At subsequent performances in the South, for instance, I was asked to omit the spanking skit (where couples spank their partner during the kiss). Sometimes I was asked to omit demonstrating how to give a hickey. Some schools objected to the Trobriand Islands kiss, which involves biting the lower lip and kissing during simulated sex. And some (but not many) objected to the shower kiss. I was able to keep the shower kiss in almost all the other southern schools simply by adding the words *And she's in the shower wearing her bathing suit.*

I learned that it's critically important to know your audience. This way you can make slight adjustments to your material and still keep everyone happy. Or almost everyone. . . . As you'll see in the chapters that follow, when directing a kissing show there are some people that you're *never* going to please.

CHAPTER TWO

WHY I WROTE
THE ART OF KISSING

I'M A LITTLE UNEASY ABOUT REVEALING the origin of my first book since doing so will make me sound less like its creator and more like the receiver of an inspired plan put into my head by the hand of fate. But setting aside these reservations is the only way to explain how I got the idea to research and write *The Art of Kissing* in the first place.

The story you're about to read about the kissing show and *The Art of Kissing*—the book that launched the show—is the result of the effect of my muse upon me. Only in this case my muse wasn't an ethereal goddess that exists only in the mind of a poet—she was a flesh-and-blood girl who lived upstairs from me when I was twenty-four.

At the time I was living in a lodging house in Brookline, Massachusetts. I had the largest studio in the building, even though by contemporary standards it was quite small. My room had southern exposure and plenty of sunlight throughout the day, with two huge windows overlooking a back alley lined with trees. It was a quiet neighborhood and perfect for me because I was writing a play about Yukio Mishima, the Japanese novelist who had killed himself in 1970. Now to understand what happened and how I met my muse, you have to visualize the ventilation grate that was on the floor in the corner of my room. Through that vent the sounds from the studio above were transmitted as if they were being broadcast by a radio. That summer a guy and girl moved into the room above me, and through that ventilation duct I couldn't help but hear them talking—and making out.

Keep in mind that in 1973 I had precipitously taken a leave of absence from Fordham College in order to devote more time to creative writing. Wanting to escape the hustle and bustle of New York, I had moved to the relative tranquility of greater Boston. It was absolutely imperative that I have peace and quiet so that I could concentrate. Naturally, those sounds from above disturbed my concentration. But they also had another effect. I hadn't even seen the girl, but I fell head over heels in love with her! Friends, it was *love at first hearing*.

I realize this may sound crazy, but it was the tone of her voice that first attracted me to her, the ironic nature of her taunts when she replied to her boyfriend and the petulant manner in which she teased him. For example, I heard the guy ask her to open the window one day, and she snapped back, "I have a better idea. Why don't we get an air conditioner?" This was precisely the kind of personality I liked in a girl, and I thought it would be great fun to have little battle of wits with someone like her.

Within a short time I had devised a unique but totally absurd strategy to accomplish my goal. I had always been interested in drama and as early as my high school days had directed my friends in amateur productions of plays.

I especially loved the theater of the absurd. In fact, in high school one of my favorite books had been Martin Esslin's *The Theatre of the Absurd* (1961). I found myself powerfully drawn to over-the-top and provocative stage comedies by Ionesco, Beckett, and Pinter more than anything.

It must have been my flair for theatrical stunts that gave me the idea that I used to meet the girl upstairs. Now, on my floor, which was the third story in the lodging house, there lived a tall man who liked to sleep with his door open in the summertime to get a breeze. He was a heavy sleeper, and I could hear him snoring in his room every afternoon. He also liked to sleep in the nude, except for his white briefs, and he would lie stretched out like a dead man on his floor. Yes, his *floor*—not his bed. For some reason he liked to sleep on the floor, maybe because it was cooler. So, to turn this setup to my advantage, I made a huge sign out of cardboard that said:

SEX CLINIC

and when this guy fell asleep and started snoring, I taped the sign up over his door.

Before long I got a sense of my upstairs neighbors' schedule and I would put up my SEX CLINIC sign whenever I expected them to return home. In this way I avoided annoying any other residents with the sign, and I only set this scenario up when I thought the couple would see it. Within a few days I got lucky and timed it just right. I was sitting in my room reading a book when I heard them mounting the creaky wooden stairs. I stole to my door and pressed my ear to it: their footsteps slowed momentarily, then continued upstairs without any comments from the pair. Had they seen it? I was dying to know, but they hadn't spoken.

As soon as they entered their room I moved to the ventilation grate. For a minute there was dead silence, and I felt disappointed. But then the girl spoke and my heart quickened at her words:

"Did you see the sex clinic sign?"

"Yeah."

Her boyfriend didn't even sound curious, but the girl had been intrigued, and just as I had hoped, this bizarre setup had piqued her imagination, if only to make her wonder about the person who had put up the sign. It had at last put me into her consciousness! And it was exactly this spark of consciousness that I planned to fan into a flame of intense interest.

An opportunity presented itself to me four days later. Sounds in the lodging house were amplified so that I could always hear footsteps above me and in the hallway. This meant that I could easily tell when the boy left for the day, either to go to school or work—I didn't know exactly where he went, I just knew that sometimes he was absent when his girlfriend was home. On this particular day the temperature had climbed into the upper eighties, or maybe it had even reached ninety or more. Neither I nor the couple upstairs had an air conditioner, so I was sweating in my room in a pair of gym shorts. I happened to go to the window, and what I saw took my breath away.

The girl was reclining on the topmost landing of the fire escape in a blue bikini and a straw hat. She was reading a magazine and didn't notice me. I stepped back into my room at once, not wanting to distract her or call attention to myself, but my mind started working overtime.

What could I do to meet her? Yes, this was the perfect time now that her boyfriend was away, but because of my love of big dramatic moments, I couldn't bring myself to simply throw open my french windows and say, "Hello!" Instinctively I felt that doing so would be the wrong way to make a memorable first impression, especially with a girl who was enjoying the privacy of her fire escape. I needed another plan of action, and I needed it quick. Whatever I did, I had to do it before her boyfriend returned. But what—what could I do?

That summer I had enrolled in a tae kwon do martial arts class in Kenmore Square, and I had a clean white karate *gi* hanging in my closet. I had also recently read several biographies of Yukio Mishima as background research for the play I was writing. Mishima had committed ritual seppuku in 1970, and his biographies described all the details of traditional Japanese suicide. Thinking this might be a good way to attract the girl's attention—and simultaneously rehearse a scene from the play I was writing—I stepped into the hall and removed a bottle of ketchup from the common refrigerator, and then I reentered my room and donned my karate *gi*. I happened to have a short plastic sword, which I had used as a prop for a theatrical performance some years earlier, and I placed this sword near the window, ready to hand. Next I poured ketchup on the front of my white jacket. Then as quietly as possible I unlocked my casement windows. With one push they opened like a french door, and I stepped onto the narrow fire escape outside my room, clutching the sword in one hand and writhing in mock agony. I fully expected that the girl would rush down the short flight of steps to attempt to save my life.

Instead, she gasped in horror and sprang back into her room! When I glanced up she was gone.

I clambered back into my studio, completely frustrated. Where had she gone? Her footsteps were pattering back and forth above me, frantically crisscrossing her floor. *What was she doing?* A moment later I heard her charge past my door and disappear downstairs.

I left my room and peered down the stairwell. The girl was talking with the landlady. I could see that she had thrown a cream-colored bathrobe over her shoulders, but I couldn't make out what she was saying. I stepped back into my doorway and waited, my heart skipping beats. Before long the girl began mounting the steps, and when she finally reached my floor I stepped out and faced her. She stopped and gawked at me as if I were a madman. I admit I must have looked ridiculous in my ketchup-covered jacket.

"Hi," I said.

The girl stood speechless before me.

She had blue eyes and blonde hair, but her face was so pale I couldn't tell whether she was frightened or amused by my appearance.

"I'm all right," I said. "I—well, I guess I just wanted to tell you I'm, err, okay."

A little tremor ran through her frame, and her eyes widened. I still couldn't tell whether she was laughing or relieved, but she said, "The landlady told me not to bother calling the police. She said you're crazy."

Then she smiled.

"Listen, my name's William Cane."

"Marcie Parker."

And then and there, dear reader, she extended her palm from under her bathrobe and we shook hands.

"Are you behind the sex clinic?"

I admitted as much.

"Why? . . . What's it all about?"

Now it was my turn to experience a little shiver of excitement. I was finally talking with her, and she was clearly curious and interested. So I came right out and told her the truth: "I wanted to meet you. I thought this would be a good way to catch your attention."

I could tell in that moment that she wasn't afraid of me, and that she didn't buy the landlady's claim that I was crazy. I realized that I had communicated with her, and that on some level she knew that I had been inspired by her. And in that first conversation she revealed that she was a student at Simmons College and that she was originally from Rhode Island. She had moved into the apartment with her boyfriend and was hoping that they could buy a condo when they earned enough money.

"My boyfriend thinks you're crazy."

"I just thought it would be a funny way to say hello."

"Next time don't make believe you're killing yourself, okay?"

After that meeting, which thrilled the daylights out of me—I had finally met her, and she was *nice*!—things progressed in a direction I never would have imagined. A few days later there was a knock on my door. When I opened it I was pleasantly surprised.

Marcie was standing there with a couple of books.

"I hear you typing sometimes," she said.

"Oh, I'm sorry about that—"

"No, no . . . it doesn't *bother* me."

"By the way, do you want to come in?"

She stepped into my room and looked around. My desk

took up most of the space in the middle of the floor so that I could take advantage of the sunlight when I was writing. Marcie sat down and told me she had a term paper that needed typing, and she wondered if I could do it.

"Typing?" I said. "Are you sure you don't want me to just *write* it for you?"

"You can write it?"

"Sure."

"But how can you do that? I mean, where would you get the research?"

"I can write about any subject, except I'm no good at economics. But anything else—literature, sociology, history—I can write about any of that. What's your paper about?"

"The Scarlet Letter."

"Did you already start it?"

She looked sheepishly at her hands. "I was going to start it this week."

"Look," I said. "Why don't you let me write it?"

She appeared momentarily flabbergasted, but when she regained her composure she agreed with my suggestion. And that's how my relationship with Marcie Parker began. Before long I was writing all her term papers, and we got to talk a couple of times a week. Eventually I realized that she was going to stay with her boyfriend, and that nothing would change that—at least not in the short term, anyway.

Then one day I was sitting in my room thinking about Marcie Parker and how I could impress her. Sure, I was writing term papers for her, but that wasn't good enough; I had to do something bigger and better, more out of the ordinary, something like that stunt where I had pretended

I was killing myself. But what could I do next that would impress her? The more I thought about it, the more I obsessed about those sounds I could hear through the vent, and that's when a wild and wonderful idea stole into my brain and I realized what I had to do: I had to write a *book* about kissing—a book that would cover every type of kiss under the sun, a book the likes of which no one had ever written before. If I could write a book like *that*, then Marcie would have to realize that it was me she needed in her life, not that guy she was living with.

Long story short, I wrote so many papers for her that I probably should have received her college degree when she graduated. A year later she moved out of town, and we eventually lost contact. But she *did* leave something behind with me, and it was as precious a gift as you could imagine—the idea for the book.

Clearly a muse doesn't have to be an immaterial goddess or a mere fantasy. When your inspiration comes from a real flesh-and-blood girl like Marcie Parker it can produce a much stronger effect, motivating you to do things you never dreamed possible. I have to thank Marcie for inspiring me to write *The Art of Kissing*, but little did I realize that the book would change my life, sending me on a series of mind-numbing cross-country excursions where I would entertain hundreds of thousands of college students. And an even more challenging muse was fated to play a major part in that show, as I will explain, but it would turn out to be a rocky road every step of the way.

CHAPTER THREE

THE BOSTON ARTS GROUP

ONE OTHER LIFE EVENT INFLUENCED ME to write a book about kissing, and the strange thing is that it happened in a theater. It occurred in 1979 when I was working as a house manager at the Boston Arts Group. Every morning I would ride my bicycle down Beacon Street into Kenmore Square in Boston, and then speed down Massachusetts Avenue and Boylston Street to the home of the most active regional theater in Massachusetts. This was without doubt the most fun place I had ever worked.

When I first arrived at the theater I wasn't employed; instead I volunteered to run the elevator. The Boston Arts Group (called BAG for short) had its headquarters in a venerable old brick building. A dance school occupied the first two floors, and we had our office on the third floor and theaters on the fourth, fifth, and sixth floors. The main stage was on the fifth floor, and it seated two hundred. The theaters on the fourth and sixth floors were smaller. My favorite space was the top floor, a cozy little theater with a capacity of only fifty, but by virtue of the fact that it was isolated from all the activity downstairs, it possessed an exotic and magical quality that I found inspirational. I saw many productions there and eventually produced two of my own plays in the space. As an elevator operator I got to meet all the important people from the theater, including Bart McCarthy, the artistic director, and his girlfriend and codirector, Vanessa Rand.

I liked volunteering at the theater so much that I would turn up like clockwork every day and stay until well past closing. BAG leased its theaters to many other production companies, so our stages were almost always active, and we offered more than three hundred productions a year. During the run of a show I usually stayed late into the evening to help close the theater. After being an elevator boy for a few weeks, I was promoted to assist the company's secretary with administrative tasks and correspondence. One afternoon Bart came into the office and sat down on my desk. He was tall and thin and had a scruffy reddish beard. He was a friendly guy but he had never sat on my desk before, so I was wondering what was up.

"Ronnie complained about you at the staff meeting today," he said.

Ronnie was one of the staff members who worked upstairs, and I was surprised that she had a complaint about me, but for some reason Bart was smiling.

"She said, 'Bill arrives late every day. He doesn't usually get here until ten in the morning. All the rest of us—myself included—have to be here at nine. I think he should be disciplined or fired if he can't be on time.'"

Bart laughed.

"'But Ronnie,' I said, 'Bill isn't on our payroll. He's a volunteer. He comes in every day and doesn't even get paid.' Ronnie was shocked. A motion was made immediately to pay you a regular weekly salary. You really do contribute to our organization, and we all enjoy working with you. So we voted to pay you $100 a week. I wish it could be more, but that's all we can afford right now."

"Wow, Bart, that's awesome! I never expected it, but I'm really happy."

"You'll get your first check next week."

"Does that mean I have to report at nine?"

He laughed.

"No, you can still come in whenever you want."

The next day Ronnie apologized, and I told her not to think about it and that I was glad to be working at the theater.

After I had been helping out for a few months, a small production company booked the fifth floor for a one-act play. This wasn't a typical booking, which would run anywhere from two to three weeks—it was only a one-day event that was promoted as a lesbian festival. I was in charge of opening and closing the theater. Within a few weeks I would be promoted to house manager, but at the time of this event I was still a general assistant, and I did odd jobs and helped almost every member of the staff from time to time. To be perfectly honest, I wasn't looking forward to being the usher—I hated doing that because it was tedious work, and ticket sales looked like they were going to amount to about two hundred people. They had a sold-out crowd on the day of their performance, and I stood in the box office collecting tickets and occasionally making a run with the elevator to bring guests up to the fifth floor. As the person in charge of the theater, I had the right to wander in and out of the house during the performance, and I often used this prerogative to watch whatever play we had at the moment, but in this instance I was bored with the show and stayed only a few minutes and then went out to the hallway to have a cigarette. Besides, the air-conditioning wasn't working properly, and it was stifling inside. But then something happened that changed my mind completely about this event, and I could never in a million years have seen it coming.

When the performance ended, everyone in the audience got up and started talking with the actors, so that the space was immediately crowded from wall to wall with lesbians. There wasn't one single man in the venue except me. I walked around picking up discarded programs, but it was a new experience for me to be surrounded by members of the opposite sex who didn't consider me in the least bit interesting, especially since most of the gals who worked at BAG flirted with me all the time. And then in the dark recesses of that theater, two of the women started kissing. One of them was leaning at a precarious angle against the wall so that she appeared to be in danger of falling. I had never seen such a passionate kiss, and I had to tear my eyes away. I continued picking up discarded ticket stubs and trash, but I couldn't help casting glances at those two young women who were putting on a show of their own.

The image of that kiss stayed with me like an indelible stamp, mixed with the bittersweet hollowness I felt when the theater finally emptied and I was left to sweep up and turn out the lights and ride my bike home in the dark. I never imagined at the time that those passionate kisses would be part of a book I would eventually write, or that they would one day lead to a related skit in the kissing show. All that was in the future. Least of all did I realize that my research for the book was destined to get me into a whole lot of trouble at the Jesuit university where I would shortly be teaching.

CHAPTER FOUR

LIP-O-SUCTION

AFTER ACTING, DIRECTING, AND HELPING out with administrative tasks as house manager of the Boston Arts Group for a couple of years, I decided to go to law school; but by the time I passed the Massachusetts bar exam in 1986, I realized that being an attorney wasn't exactly my cup of tea. I worked as a trial lawyer with my friend Bryant Alvarez, who eventually went on to become a renowned elder law attorney, but I retired from the practice of law after six weeks.

Immediately after putting all my case files into permanent storage, and without any regrets about the three years that I had devoted to studying law, I threw myself wholeheartedly into a new career teaching English at Boston College. In addition to teaching during the regular academic year, I also taught a summer school vocabulary-building class. James A. Woods, SJ, the dean of the summer school, was a mastermind of marketing, and each summer he enrolled hundreds of exceptional high school students from around the world. Since I had developed a reputation for teaching an enjoyable class, word spread far and wide, even back to Puerto Rico, where many of the summer school students hailed from, and I often had more than a hundred students enrolled in my class. It was held in an auditorium that resembled a movie theater, with a seating capacity close to three hundred.

What made my class so different was the way that I taught vocabulary by assigning students to participate in skits where they would use the new words. The course quickly turned into an acting class. By having an opportunity to use these vocabulary words in enjoyable little scenarios, they learned proper pronunciation and usage, and some of them told me that they still remembered the words decades later. I did my utmost to make everyone feel welcomed and special. Those who really didn't like to speak in public worked the lights and video cameras, and they even helped with makeup and costumes. These classes became full-scale theatrical productions, and the last two weeks of the semester were spent rehearsing the skits. Then on the next-to-last day we videotaped the entire show, and on the last day of the semester we watched our production on the auditorium movie screen.

So how could this good-natured fun lead to any trouble? You would think I'd be receiving accolades from the university for teaching so many students in an engaging way. But the problem I ran into stemmed from the fact that I tended to forget that I was at a Catholic college. Father Woods was such an easygoing supervisor that I found it hard to remember that he had a specific reputation to uphold both inside and outside the institution.

In 1989 when I announced that I was researching a book about kissing, my students appeared mildly amused. I gave them extra credit if they completed my questionnaire because the survey contained 208 questions and amounted to a significant writing exercise. At the same time, I published the questions in *Book News*, an academic journal, which netted me some good responses from people who could write a coherent paragraph, something many of my students found too challenging. Meanwhile, I collected about twenty-five surveys from my summer class, and to be fair they did have some helpful responses.

Each week I also gave them a pen-and-paper vocabulary quiz, and while the test was being administered, I sat in front monitoring the class. Now, one thing that always set this class apart from my regular fall and spring classes was that the students were younger: they were sixteen-year-olds who had completed their third year of high school with a B-plus average. But the fact that they were young and that the class was offered in the summer tended to encourage them to act casually and joke around with me more. I still recall vividly how one particular girl from Puerto Rico, Lilliana, treated the class like a game instead of an academic endeavor. Ritchie, one of the Boston boys, quickly became her constant companion, and, bless his heart, the fellow always had a smile on his face.

Before the vocabulary test was finished Lilliana approached my desk, test in hand. I thought she was going to turn it in early, but that wasn't what she had in mind.

"Professor, did you hear about lip-o-suction?"

She had spoken in a subdued voice, but because everybody was taking a test, the room was quiet and her comment carried all the way to the back. A few people started giggling.

Now, years later, reflecting back on what happened, I know that I should have asked her to return to her seat. But back then I wasn't thinking completely rationally.

I had such blind enthusiasm for my book project that I threw all caution to the wind and let her continue.

She plunked her test facedown on my desk and stood in front of me, pointing at a crude illustration drawn on the back of the page. It depicted a boy and girl kissing, a close-up of their mouths and lips.

"The boy kisses the *upper* lip," she explained. "The girl kisses the *lower* lip . . . See?"

Yes, I could clearly see that she had drawn the kiss as described.

"Then they reverse," she added. "The boy kisses the lower lip, the girl kisses the upper lip."

Now the class was in chaos. No one was paying attention to the test. Everyone was looking at Lilliana and laughing at her description. Nothing like this had ever happened in my class before, but it was going to get even worse.

"Me and Ritchie can demonstrate it for you."

I couldn't believe what I had just heard. That's why I didn't react fast enough to stop what happened next.

Lilliana turned and beckoned to Ritchie. He was a sheepish boy with tousled blond locks who resembled Steve McQueen. He seemed to be hypnotized by her. Responding immediately to her request, but without any sign of haste, he ambled up to the front of the room and smiled. In one swift motion, the girl embraced Ritchie and turned him to face her. Now they were standing profile position in front of my desk so that the entire class could see the action of their lips. Friends, at that moment I was learning exactly how to stage the kissing demonstrations in my kissing show—which was still two years away—and they were doing it all without rehearsal or direction.

Jaws dropped, girls gasped, boys guffawed, and the entire crowd began laughing as Lilliana kissed Ritchie's lower lip, while he, in turn, kissed her upper lip. Then the two lovebirds reversed: she kissed his upper lip, and he kissed her lower lip. Back and forth they went—upper lip, lower lip, upper lip, lower lip . . . but now the crowd was doing more than laughing; they were screaming, literally howling at the antics of these two kids.

When I think back about the way I simply stood watching them, I realize how crazily I acted—or *failed* to act. As the teacher I had an obligation to keep people focused and on track. But I didn't. I felt just as amused by this romantic demonstration as my class, and I made no move to put a stop to it.

In the middle of this chaotic scene, the rear door banged open and in marched Bernard Klaus, the sociology instructor. He was about fifty and was wearing horn-rimmed spectacles and a shirt and tie. No jacket. His skin had the consistency of a soggy pancake, and when he saw the spectacle unfolding in front of the room, his face turned vivid pink. Right then and there I knew I was a dead man.

"Can you keep it down in here?"

"Yes, okay," I said.

He left without another word, the kissing demonstrators returned to their seats, and I eventually collected the vocabulary tests and went home. The next day I got a phone call from Cheryl, the summer school secretary.

"Can you stop in to see Dean Woods tomorrow?"

I had a premonition that this wasn't going to be good. Father Woods was a tall man of about sixty, and when I entered his office he greeted me with a wave to the chair in front of his massive desk.

"I heard a story from Bernie Klaus that I couldn't believe. So I spoke with a few people from your class, and they confirmed what he said. Don't try to deny it. He saw two students making out! People were screaming. One of the students I talked with is an older woman."

Ouch! I remembered that we did have an adult in the class. And I knew she wasn't one of the people laughing with glee at the lip-o-suction demonstration.

"I didn't ask them to do it, Father," I began. "I told them that I was researching a book I'm writing—a serious sociological study about romantic kissing—a scholarly work with footnotes and a bibliography, by the way." This was pure exaggeration. The book would never have footnotes or a bibliography. "They just spontaneously started doing the kiss after one girl drew a picture of . . . of a kiss called lip-o-suction on the back of her vocabulary test. And I made them stop as soon as I could. I didn't let it get out of hand."

"But Klaus said it was so loud he couldn't concentrate next door. First of all, this is a Jesuit school, and this kind of behavior would not please the president of the university. If he heard about it, well, I could get in trouble myself. Second, you can't let your students disrupt the other teachers."

"Yes, sir."

"This is a friendly warning."

"Thank you, sir."

But this was just the first bombshell to explode at Boston College. My only consolation after that meeting with Dean Woods was that I was now poised to write the book. I had enough survey replies from my students and a few thousand other respondents to complete all the chapters, so I told myself that this was what I had to do: write the book and stop getting into trouble in class. Just dial it down at school and your job will be secure, and before you know it you'll be a published author. The furthest thing from my mind was the possibility that the book itself would lead to more big trouble at the very school where I had already been reprimanded.

CHAPTER FIVE

THE KISSING SHOW

"PROFESSOR CANE?"

"Yes?"

"Author of *The Art of Kissing*?"

"Yes."

"The reason I'm calling is that I'm a resident assistant at Boston College and I was wondering if you, er . . . talk about your book?"

"If I *talk* about it?"

"I mean, do you speak to groups about it?"

"Well, it was just published, so—"

"I think a lot of students would be very interested." The girl on the line laughed. "Do you think you might like to talk with them here at Boston College?"

It didn't take me two seconds to decide.

"Sure."

And with that one word, I sealed my fate. Things would never be the same for me. That conversation changed my life because before I got off the phone with the young woman, I asked her a leading question.

"Do you have any friends who might be willing to participate in the presentation by demonstrating some of the kisses from my book?"

This tickled her funny bone, and she giggled again.

"That's a good idea," she said. "I'll try to round up a few couples."

And it was that little arrangement—having the girl round up a few couples to *demonstrate* the kisses—that changed everything.

The year was 1991, and for better or worse, I was about to embark on a venture that would take me to almost every state in the union, as well as Canada and Europe, and bring me a great deal of wanted—and unwanted—media attention. I would soon be traveling from one city to the next with a small bag of props and a fifty-minute show that included all the kisses in my book. I would appear before so many audiences that I would sometimes lose track of what city I was in, and many times television crews would show up to record the event for local, national, and international news stations. I was on my way to directing thousands of young people in how to do the french kiss, the biting kiss, the vacuum kiss, the group kiss, the upside-down kiss, and many more. It wasn't long before my life was taken over by the kissing show and the hundreds of thousands of young people clamoring to see it.

Over the years while working on the show, I've appeared on hundreds of radio and television programs. Reporters and producers contacted me after they came across my book. Having written an entire book on kissing was enough to get them interested, but when they found out that I also directed a kissing show at colleges and universities, they usually became all agog over the story.

"What do you mean, you direct a *kissing* show?"

This is the first question they asked. What is a kissing

show? What goes on during such an event? And where did you ever get the idea to do something like that?

Before I tell you exactly what happened during that first kissing show at Boston College, I have to say that in many ways I feel that the show, the book, and the college lecture tour weren't my idea at all. Yes, I wrote the book, and I agreed to do that first presentation for the resident assistant at Boston College, and it sure enough was me who boarded a thousand airplane flights to travel all over the country to direct kissing demonstrations at four hundred colleges. But when I stop and think about it, the whole kit and caboodle seems to have dropped into my lap without my really having done much but accept it all like a gift from fate. Just like a tulip doesn't have much choice in the matter once it's watered and receives sunlight—it grows without any thought—in the same way, I received my water and sunlight, you might say, from the positive encouragement I received when students like the Boston College resident assistant implored me to speak at their schools.

Over the years there have been literally hundreds of these students who have patted me on the back and welcomed me to their campuses, and when you receive this kind of encouragement, it certainly does shape your behavior. I'm getting a little ahead of myself here, but when you have hundreds and sometimes thousands of cheering students in an audience, it feels like a drug as you stand in front of them and talk about something you love. It's an addictive experience. You want to do it over and over again. So, I have to say that the first show really came to me through that phone call, and while I *did* make the suggestion about having student demonstrators, I think anyone in my place would have done the same thing. I'm not trying to be modest here, but I feel that the show was generated less by my initiative and more by the overwhelming demand expressed by college students who seemed to create the performance through their irrepressible enthusiasm for kissing. It's as if all their pent-up sexual energy reached out through the ether, seeking a vehicle to embody it onstage—and there I was, in the right place, at the right time, and with the right book—ready, willing, and able to put all their kissing fantasies onstage. And I'm not complaining, either! It has been a wild and exhilarating journey every step of the way.

With that as the backdrop, I'll tell you exactly what happened and what mistakes I made in that first Boston College performance.

The first mistake I made was telling my girlfriend about it. By this point, I had been teaching for two years in the English department and in the Boston College summer experience, so I was used to speaking in front of an audience. I had also spent a few years working as an actor at the Boston Arts Group theater, and during college I had been the president of the Fulton Debating Society. So I had a lot of experience as a speaker, and I wasn't nervous about addressing a group of college students, especially if they were voluntarily attending my presentation. But when I told my girlfriend, Judy Youngson, about it, she offered to drive me to the event, and that made me a little nervous. Suddenly I wasn't simply going to be talking in front of a roomful of strangers, which I could do with ease; now I was going to be talking in front of my girlfriend, and if I happened to make a fool of myself—which was highly likely—she would remember it for the rest of her life and would probably remind me of it every time I saw her.

The good thing about Judy's offer to drive me, however, was the fact that I'm usually not on time for my appointments. If I had to get there by myself, I would most likely have been late, but after she offered to drive me, I had to be ready on time when she came to pick me up.

Now, one thing you should know about me is that I'm an avid reader. By this I mean that before I even went to college I had read more than a thousand books, including almost all the works of Nietzsche, Sartre, Camus, Ionesco, Rimbaud, Baudelaire, and hundreds more. So when I prepared for this first lecture, I wrote my entire speech out word for word in a bookish way, and I included plenty of quotes from *The Art of Kissing*. I also rehearsed for hours, even going so far as to walk back and forth in my studio as if I were in front of an audience. At this point in the show's history I didn't have any props—that would all come later—but I did have a twenty-page outline, which I stapled like a booklet so that I could hold it in my hand to guide me as I gave the presentation.

As promised, Judy arrived ninety minutes before the show was supposed to start, and we went down to her car, a four-door sedan. Even in those days I was a terrible driver, and I knew it, so I was glad that she was behind the wheel. As you'll see later, things would get dangerous whenever I tried to drive a car. This first performance was in October, and it was already dark by the time we arrived in Chestnut Hill at the campus of Boston College. Judy drove up the steep driveway to the O'Connell House Student Union, where the event had a scheduled start time of eight p.m. I was nervous about where Judy planned to sit, and I was hoping it wouldn't be a distraction to see her in the audience.

As an undergraduate in the early 1980s I had founded the Boston College Radio Theater with a friend, and I had already directed more than a hundred half-hour radio plays. So what I was looking forward to more than anything was the opportunity to direct the volunteer couples that Jackie Watkins, the resident assistant, had rounded up for me. When I entered the student union, Jackie was already there. A prepossessing young woman with a warm smile, she introduced me to the first volunteer couple and promised that three more couples were on their way. Then she led us into a private rehearsal room off the main hallway. The students in the first volunteer couple seemed excited to be in the event. Soon the other volunteers arrived, and I was fortunate that all four couples looked terrific—wearing business casual attire, their hair combed and styled—and they were easy to direct.

I had only half an hour to rehearse my volunteers. I began by thanking them for showing up, and then I gave them an overview of the show.

"I'm going to talk for about ten minutes at the beginning and read some quotations from my book. During this time you'll be sitting onstage. Then we'll ask you to stand and we'll do the first demonstration, a simple lip kiss. Why don't you stand now and show me a lip kiss."

Obediently, they stood and shyly turned toward each other.

"Go ahead," I encouraged them. "Just do a simple lip kiss, nothing advanced right at the outset. There'll be plenty of time for that later!"

They giggled and kissed. The beauty of having four couples is that each one performs the demonstration slightly differently: some will do a lip kiss sensuously;

other couples will do the ear kiss better, with the girl getting weak in the knees; still other couples will excel at the neck kiss, where the boys kiss the neck of their partner. My audiences always had *something* interesting and visually exciting to look at—if one couple wasn't catching their attention, they could turn their gaze left or right and see what the next couple was doing. In this way there was never a dull moment, and the demonstrations always had the potential to captivate the crowd. This is also why I never pressured my volunteers during rehearsal: I simply described each kiss to them and watched what they did, realizing that at least one couple would probably be fabulous and exciting for the audience. There were thirty kisses in all, and the entire show took about an hour— depending on how fast they kissed.

The second mistake I made during that first show was that I didn't request that the volunteers have an early enough call time, and as a result I was a little rushed in rehearsal. I soon learned that I needed to ask volunteers to arrive at least ninety minutes before curtain to ensure that I had enough time to run through all the demonstrations. But in those days the show was simpler and I had less to tell the volunteers, so it all worked out in the end.

Shortly after eight o'clock my demonstrators and I walked into the main hall. This space was a large public area, at the back of which a sweeping wooden stairway rose and divided into two flights, like in the *Gone With the Wind* scene where Rhett Butler leans Scarlett back for a kiss and then carries her up the stairs. My demonstrators looked a little pale when they saw how many students had packed into the venue. It was filled to overflowing with about 250 Boston College students, some sitting on folding chairs, but most camped out on the floor and on the flight of steps. I was delightfully surprised by the turnout, and I was even more pleased when I smiled at the crowd and didn't see Judy anywhere. I could relax and do my thing without feeling that she was scrutinizing everything critically, even though I felt sure she was somewhere in the room, probably in the back, trying to remain inconspicuous. *I'm in luck*, I thought . . . and I breathed a silent thank-you.

Jackie introduced me, reading a short paragraph that I had written for her. The audience was receptive to my initial remarks, in which I mentioned the book and the research I had conducted. I then regaled the crowd with five minutes of quotations, reading directly from my book, which I held along with my voluminous outline. A few years later I would learn that reading isn't too effective with audiences, and that it's better to have the material memorized so that you can deliver it in a more natural way. Before long I knew all the quotations by heart, and I would simply hold the book and glance down occasionally to give the impression that I was reading. But for that first show I had to follow my outline because I didn't want to omit any of the demonstrations and I wanted to do them in a prearranged order, which I felt would have the most impact: beginning with the lip kiss, moving on to more advanced techniques like the biting kiss, the sliding kiss, the ear and neck kiss, and concluding with the most exciting demonstrations—the group kiss, the vacuum kiss, and finally the most intimate demonstration of all, the french kiss.

The audience stayed with us throughout the whole presentation, laughing, listening, and leaning forward, devouring everything that I said and especially everything the demonstrators did. After the show I was elated when we received thunderous applause. Jackie Watkins thanked me warmly and gave me a gift certificate to Pizzeria Uno. Judy emerged from the crowd and said she enjoyed the presentation too. On the drive home she gave me a tip that helped me improve the show.

"I noticed that they got into it more when music was playing," she said.

I had used a boom box for background music during a few of the skits, and then near the end of the show we used it again for the music kiss, which involves demonstrators kissing on the beat to fast rock music. This feedback helped me decide to use more music in the show, and I eventually printed a detailed music cue sheet that I would rehearse with the music director at all future schools.

The final problem with this performance is that it almost went too well. In other words, there was no way that this streak of good luck could continue: when things go this well, the only real direction you can go is down. From this point on, things were going to get unmanageable very quickly, and I would rarely have a performance as successful as this first one; instead, major problems were going to crop up at almost all my future gigs. But on that night I didn't know that the show was going to have legs. I thought, *okay, I've done a presentation based on my book, we've had a few laughs, and that'll be the end of it.* Later that week I treated Judy to dinner at Uno Pizzeria, feeling rather proud of myself.

Meanwhile, the buzz generated by this event was spreading like wildfire from Boston College to other New England schools.

CHAPTER SIX

MEDIA FRENZY

TO MY IMMENSE SURPRISE, I RECEIVED A call one day from Marla Glading, my literary agent, and she told me that translation rights to the book had been bought by a foreign publisher. I don't think I ever expected that to happen, but I was naturally thrilled, especially when she told me the terms of the deal.

"It's a German publisher, and they're going to bring the book out in three different editions: a trade paperback, a hardcover, and a smaller mass-market paperback for sale in airports and convenience stores. The deal is for . . . are you sitting down?"

I sat down.

"Yes. Tell me."

"Thirty thousand dollars!"

"Thirty *thousand*?"

"Can you believe it?"

I almost fainted. This was 1991, mind you, when $30,000 would be the equivalent of $60,000 in today's currency. Remember, too, that I was living in a rent-controlled apartment and my weekly rent was only $135. Like many creative people who focus more on their work than on amassing a fortune at the start of their careers, I was living in a state of near destitution, but luckily my expenses were so low I was able to scrape by on my meager income. Suddenly I was going to have so much money my lifestyle would almost certainly change.

A few weeks later I received a letter from my editor congratulating me on the German sale and telling me that three other foreign publishers had picked up the book: South Korea, Italy, and Portugal. Within a few months, more phone calls from my agent and congratulatory letters from my editor . . . and before the year was out we had sold the book to twenty foreign publishers. It was published in so many different translations that publishers started getting careless with typography and accuracy, and one of the Danish editions even came out with my name misspelled on the cover! I fired off a letter to my editor, but there's not much you can do when the people printing your books speak another language and don't have any obligation to show you a preproduction copy before they rush it onto bookshelves. *The Art of Kissing* became an international bestseller and was featured in a *Publishers Weekly* article, the trade magazine for the book industry. Naturally my agent, editor, and publisher were all glowing, and so was I.

But unbeknownst to me, things were happening that would soon turn my happy world into a nightmarish farce. I didn't know it at the time, but my publicist at St. Martin's had taken out an advertisement for the book in *Radio-TV Reports*, a monthly magazine that circulated to almost all the radio and television stations in the country. Before long my phone was ringing off the hook with interview requests from radio and television producers. It began innocently enough like this:

"Hello, is this William Cane?"

"Yes."

"This is the producer from the *Tomorrow Is Today* radio program in Dallas, Texas. How are you?"

Naturally, with my ego, I was elated.

"I'm excited you're calling me."

"We'd like you to come on our show at three o'clock New York time this afternoon and do a half-hour interview about your book."

"Great!"

"Can you do it?"

"Count me in!"

In those days I was an eager beaver. I loved getting invited on radio and television programs. You might say I was a hog for attention. I'm not sure why I turned out this way, but I'll tell you a funny story that illustrates just how eager for attention I was and always have been. When I was seventeen, right after I graduated from high school, my father announced that he had tickets to a television game show in which St. Peter's College in Jersey City would be competing. It was a quiz show, like the $64,000 question program, and he worked at the college in the guidance department, which is how he had received the tickets. He said I could go with him if I was interested. Of course I wanted to go. I happened to know that when the contest was over, the cameras turned around toward the studio audience for about thirty or forty seconds during the closing credits. It occurred to me that this would be my first opportunity to appear on television—provided I was lucky enough to be seen in the audience.

Well, you can bet that I was going to do everything

in my power to make sure that I was seen. I wore my London Fog raincoat to the studio because even though it was a clear night and even though it was a black-and-white program I knew this coat's light-beige color would increase my visibility. I sat in my seat thoroughly bored all through that half-hour taping session. I had absolutely no interest in the show itself; all I cared about were those precious few moments when I would have a chance to appear on camera. But how was I going to be noticed in that audience? There were two hundred people sitting in the studio with me, and I knew I had to do something to increase my visibility. So when the contest was over and they turned on the house lights and the television cameras swung around to view us, I leaped to my feet and began waving my arms over my head. Everyone else was sitting down applauding, but as those cameras panned across the crowd, I stood on my toes and continued waving like a maniac, determined to be seen. I didn't care if I was blocking the view of the people sitting behind me. This was my moment to shine! A week later when the episode aired I was overjoyed to see that the camera had indeed caught me, plainly visible and waving my arms back and forth—the only person standing in that entire audience. Why, I wondered, had I been the only one who leaped out of his seat? Didn't *everybody* want to be the focus of attention?

My need for attention was almost insane. I would do anything for media coverage, so after my book's publication date I was secretly thrilled that I was receiving calls two and three times a week to appear on radio shows. The interviews were always extremely easy to do; after all, I had written an entire book on kissing, and the questions were always the same: Why did you write a book about kissing? How did you do your research? What's the most surprising thing you discovered? What's the biggest mistake people make when kissing? How can you do a perfect kiss? These questions and simple variations on them were asked time and again, and before long I could complete media interviews almost without thinking. But I always had fun doing them because I was talking about myself and my research.

The publicist at St. Martin's also mailed me newspaper and magazine clippings, which she collected and photocopied for me, and these stories usually had something positive to say about the book. I was amazed how lucky I had gotten. Most authors don't receive much publicity, don't get reviewed, and never become translated into other languages. Yet here I was receiving all this attention—it was almost unbelievable.

I was so busy being a publicity hound that I hadn't talked with one of my best friends, Jessica Beaton, in a few months. She had moved into a new apartment with her boyfriend and was living in an affluent section of Brookline that I rarely visited, near the birthplace and childhood home of John F. Kennedy. So I hit on a crazy scheme to get her attention and make her call *me*. I sent a letter to the editor of the town newspaper, *The Tab*, asking whether they might want to do a feature story about a local lad who had written a book about kissing. Not surprisingly they contacted me immediately, keenly interested in the story; in fact, they wanted to send a photographer to take my photo that very afternoon.

Shortly before the photo shoot I went across the street and bought a pack of cigarettes. I also put on my white lab coat—not my ketchup-stained karate jacket—which I had saved from my college chemistry class. When the photographer arrived, he seemed happy to have a subject who was a little out of the ordinary. What he didn't know was that I had exerted considerable effort to make sure that I didn't look normal. I had messed up my hair and donned a long white lab coat to look like a mad scientist, and I started chain-smoking cigarettes. He loaded his camera and we went downstairs. I proceeded to walk back and forth along Beacon Street like a lunatic while he took about a hundred shots.

A few days later I was pleased to see my photograph staring back at me from the front page of the newspaper—wearing my lab coat and smoking a cigarette, my hair askew, a maniacal look on my face. The headline read, "Local Author Writes Kissing Manual."

I knew Jessica read the paper religiously, and sure enough, that afternoon the phone rang and I heard her delightful voice.

"You nut!"

I laughed.

"You don't smoke, do you?"

"No. I quit a few years ago."

"Then why—?"

"Don't you know? I wanted you to see me and get back in touch. I've missed talking with you. I got invited to go to New York to be on television, and I'm a nervous wreck."

I wasn't really nervous, but I liked her to *think* I was, because she always gave me friendly advice about how to deal with things that were happening in my life. And a lot of crazy things were happening. I felt in some ways that my young life had been swept out from under my feet by all this interest in the kissing book. I was being interviewed all the time: if it wasn't a radio show, it was a television interview, and more often than not I had to travel out of town for the television programs. Now I was going to New York to be on *Donahue*, one of the biggest talk shows in the country. And he was an incisive and unpredictable interviewer. Honestly, for this one I *was* a little nervous.

But before I get to my *Donahue* appearance and all the trouble it caused me, I should explain what happened when the kissing show caught the attention of other Boston schools.

CHAPTER SEVEN

BOSTON SCHOOLS

WITHIN A MATTER OF WEEKS AFTER DOING that first show in 1991 at Boston College, I received invitations to speak at Babson, Northeastern, Boston University, and Simmons. The second show I directed was at Babson, and it was the first school that I would speak at where I didn't teach. I felt I had to be on my best behavior and maintain a professional attitude. I was somewhat of a nervous wreck before the show, thinking about all the things that could go wrong to embarrass me.

One of the students on the entertainment committee picked me up in a Volkswagen and drove me to the campus, which is in Wellesley, Massachusetts. The school was in a nice neighborhood, and we arrived as the sun was setting. The campus looked eerily deserted. Inside the venue, one of the teaching buildings, it was also quiet, and all the classrooms were empty. I chatted with my driver as he led me to the room where I would be speaking.

"What kind of school is Babson?"

"A business school mostly."

"And what are the popular majors?"

"Business, finance, and economics."

I didn't say much after that. I felt totally out of my element as I was led into a medium-size classroom that could hold about fifty students. This was a much smaller venue than O'Connell House, but my main concern wasn't the turnout; that was the responsibility of the host. I was worried about the nature of the audience I would be facing. I had never taken a business course in my life. Truth be told, I had no interest in business, and I didn't know what these students expected from me.

After a few minutes three couples showed up, and I had to rehearse them right there in the same room where we would be doing the performance. I didn't like doing that because people who showed up early for the event would see the rehearsal. I asked my host to keep the doors closed until we finished rehearsing. When we finally let the audience into the room, it turned out to be a smaller crowd than my first show, only about thirty students this time. They were polite and listened attentively as I ran though my introduction and told a few jokes. I could see right away that I would have no trouble communicating with them: business students they might be, but they were still young people in their teens and twenties, and like young people all over America, they had a healthy interest in the subject of kissing and making out. The main difference between this group and the first crowd was that here the students were better dressed, most of them wearing business casual attire, and their reactions were more reserved— they laughed but they didn't scream; they smiled but they didn't break up into uncontrollable laughter like at Boston College; and when I got into the description of each kiss before the demonstrations, they almost looked like they wanted to take notes, they were so attentive and studious.

Babson taught me my first important lesson about speaking on the college lecture circuit: I learned that each school has a slightly different spirit and esprit de corps. At Boston College it was a relaxed party spirit, whereas at Babson it was a reserved and analytic frame of mind. And soon I would discover that every school in the Boston area had different expectations when you spoke to them. At each school I had to adapt on the fly, so to speak, changing my presentation slightly to communicate effectively with the audience. This was one of the challenges of speaking at different colleges, and one of the things I enjoyed about the job: it was never dull, always slightly different, and the people I worked with and spoke to were always able to teach me a little about themselves, just as I shared a little about myself and a lot about kissing with each new audience.

After the presentation a few students came up to me and asked questions, wanting to know where they could buy my book. We had a nice interaction, and once again I was given a gift certificate to a local restaurant, this time Vinny's Pizzeria. I loved Vinny's, so I was quite happy with myself.

A few weeks later I was invited to speak at Northeastern. It was so close to where I lived that I could walk there in twenty minutes, but I took a cab because I had some props and the boom box to carry. Over the years I would speak about five or six times at Northeastern, but the first time was the easiest. The students were friendly, and they accepted all the skits and demonstrations with the kind of good humor that makes a speaker love what he's doing. By this time word about the show had spread throughout the Boston area, and the entertainment committee at Northeastern did a good job of putting up flyers for the event, so we had about two hundred in attendance. One of the students from the entertainment committee drove me home, and as he did he asked me whether I had an agent.

"Most of our speakers, including the comedians and the bands, have booking agents."

"No, I don't have one."

"It's a really good show."

"Thanks!"

Once again I received a gift certificate to Pizzeria Uno, so I was happy, but that night I mused over what the student from the entertainment committee had said about an agent. I was starting to wonder whether I should have an agent too. But I didn't know where to look for one or how to get one interested in my presentation.

Later that semester I also spoke at Boston University, and again I was welcomed with enthusiasm. I had a liberal audience that yelled and cheered at the demonstration of the first kiss, and they continued to respond with enthusiasm throughout the rest of the performance. Looking back on it now, I realize that I had begun to develop an inflated sense of my ability as a speaker because of these initial successes. Doing kissing shows was different from teaching an English class; the speaking part was similar to delivering an academic lecture, but the subject matter was so much more interesting that I didn't have to work to keep the attention of the crowds. I had a microphone at Northeastern and Boston University, and that also made it easier to hold the attention of the audience and direct the people where I wanted them to focus.

But I was in for a shock at the next school.

Simmons College was so close to where I lived that I walked to it in ten minutes. It was in a nice area near the Gardner Museum. There was a park across the street from the campus, and it looked like it was going to be a relaxing show for me. But a cloud was hanging over the event and I didn't even recognize it when I was given a big hint about the trouble to come. The girl who was my contact in the student activities board told me something that should have at least roused my curiosity, but I didn't pay much attention to it because I was concerned about finishing my sound check.

"A few feminists have complained about the show," she said.

I smiled and said that I was sorry to hear that, especially since I had a lot of radical feminist friends and acquaintances from my law school days when I had worked with a campaign to pass legislation in Cambridge and had met Andrea Dworkin and Catharine MacKinnon. It never crossed my mind that feminists could pose a problem for a show like this.

But right in the middle of the performance, four girls began marching quietly in the back of the audience, which consisted of about a hundred students sitting on the gym floor and in folding chairs that had been set up for them. The protesters didn't bother me at first. I couldn't read their signs and I didn't even know they were protesting. They were probably the most well-behaved protesters I had ever encountered. I had personally been more raucous and annoying with my feminist friends when we picketed Alan Dershowitz's deli in Cambridge in 1988. But as the show came to a conclusion, I noticed that some of the people in the audience were becoming distracted and even agitated by these gals marching with signs.

"You better leave right away," the girl from the entertainment committee said. "Our office had planned to buy you dinner, but I'm afraid that it might be better to go home now. We don't know what these protesters might do, either to us, our property, or—I hesitate to say it—to you personally. We have an armored car waiting outside."

"An armored car?"

"We took that precaution because this isn't the first time we've had to make a clandestine escape with one of our speakers."

Slightly unnerved, I packed up my props double time and followed my entertainment committee escorts through a narrow passageway to the campus parking lot. We arrived at the armored car without incident, but as we were driving away a couple of protesters spotted us and made a beeline for the vehicle. They were brandishing placards on sticks and waving their arms. One of the signs read "UNFAIR TO WOMEN!" and the other "GO HOME!" These protests didn't make sense to me, since I had always thought of myself as compatible with feminists. Over the next few years, however, such protests would increase in frequency at my events, as well as at other events on college campuses, so much so that the kissing program had to curtail its run on the lecture circuit. But on that night I had no prevision of these future consequences of student protests. All I was thinking about was whether our car would make it safely to the street. I felt thankful when the protesters didn't throw anything at us, and seconds later we sped down the Fenway into the night.

I had made my first quick getaway from a kissing show, but sorry to say it wouldn't be my last.

CHAPTER EIGHT

DONAHUE

IT ALWAYS ANNOYED ME HOW MY STUDENTS seemed more impressed by my television appearances than by my books. One day Kevin Moore explained it to me, and the way he put it made me realize that I shouldn't be annoyed; instead, I should feel sorry for them.

"Most college students consider television more impressive than any other credential," he said. "So when you design your flyers, always mention that you were on nearly every major television talk program."

How right he was! When my students learned that I had been invited to appear on *Donahue*, they could hardly believe it. They begged me to let them see a tape of the segment. I felt kind of sorry for them and wished that they would sometimes get similarly excited about books.

But my father had a completely different reaction. "Be careful when you go on his show," he warned. "He's crafty. He'll get you to say and do things you'll regret."

I found it amusing to hear this from a man who had cautioned me about reading Nietzsche, and yet I considered the advice unsettling, too, since my father was a psychologist and presumably had some insight into people and their motivation. I was depressed on the flight to New York, thinking of all the things that could go awry and embarrass me in front of a national audience. I'm the type of person who worries about things in advance, but when the day came to arrive at the studio, I snapped back to my normal cheerful and confident self.

In the dressing room I had a chance to chat with the other guests, one of whom was a psychologist who used hypnosis to help people with life problems. He was about forty-five and, like me, wearing a suit and tie. It made me feel more at home to be a guest alongside this professional. The producers had asked him to hypnotize a married couple and give them a posthypnotic suggestion to enhance their kissing enjoyment.

The married couple were in their forties. They seemed like nice people, but they also appeared uncommonly shy. Why had they allowed themselves to be roped into this silly affair? Producers are forever dreaming up mindless business for guests to perform. But you have to play along if you want to be on television, and my publisher was keen for me to be on as many television programs as possible. Ironically, it wasn't the St. Martin's Press publicist who had gotten me this shot on *Donahue*. I did it myself, and it was easy: I simply mailed Phil Donahue a brief letter describing my book and suggesting that his audience might find me interesting. A couple of days later one of his producers called and invited me to be a guest. At the time, *Donahue* was the number-one daytime talk show, but he had a reputation for being edgy and doing outlandish things, which is why my father had warned me that I was headed for trouble. I refrained from telling my dad that I had invited myself into the situation in the first place, and that there was no way I was going to turn down this opportunity.

In addition to the hypnotist and the married couple, a vivacious young woman joined us in the dressing room. She had written a book about how to maximize your enjoyment of sex, and she impressed everyone as a bubbly and talkative person who would clearly appeal to Phil Donahue's love of good-natured and provocative entertainment.

While we were talking with each other Donahue entered the room, jacketless and wearing pants with suspenders. He told us what to expect.

"I want you to know that without you there would be no show. You should not be awed by my presence or by the fact that we're on television. You each have something important to contribute, and *you* are the heart and soul of the program. I'm relying on you. Also keep in mind that things will move quickly. Before you know it, the show will be over. So make a point of saying what you want and communicating your message—only *you* can do that. I'll do my best to prompt you, but in the midst of a live taping things get hectic, so take this responsibility seriously and make sure that you say what you want, okay?"

We all agreed to do our best, and he nodded and left the dressing room. Shortly thereafter we were ushered into a brightly illuminated television studio where about two hundred people sat scrutinizing our every move. For me, this was no big deal. I regularly spoke to a class of about this size at Boston College, and I knew how to handle an audience like this. The television cameras didn't bother me or intimidate me either. The only thing I found annoying—or frustrating, really—was the fact that Phil

Donahue was in the room. He was the only one walking around with a microphone, so he had total control. I was used to being in that situation in the classroom and also when directing the kissing show. In those situations, I was the one with the microphone and I was in charge, so it was a little vexing to have to sit back and let someone else lead the parade.

When it came time for our segment, the psychologist, who had hypnotized the couple off camera, explained that the man and woman were now ready to do a kissing demonstration. I stood up to tell them what to do.

"Is it okay with you, Doctor?" Donahue asked.

The hypnotist looked surprised at the question.

I was surprised too, because this was exactly what the producers had told us we would be doing, so of course it should be okay.

"Yes," the hypnotist said. "The couple has already received their posthypnotic suggestion."

"Okay," I said. "We're ready to go . . . I don't know *where* we're going, but we're ready to begin the demonstration."

And here I simply gave a brief instruction to the man and woman on how to do lip-o-suction. It was a good choice for this public display of affection: there was no tongue involved and the studio cameras could capture close-ups of all the action. I also knew it was a popular kiss with young people. My sixteen-year-old summer school students had proved as much.

Before I talk about the rest of the program, I need to interject a note about the way you feel when you're invited on a television or radio show. As I explained earlier, I was a media hound and I loved all the attention. Performing in front of an audience affected me like a drug, and the rush I got from being in a studio with hundreds of people was addictive. If you're not intimidated by public speaking, you want to do it again and again. But it's all a matter of feeding your ego: you lose perspective and think that *your* ideas are the most important ones in the world. A strange temporary megalomania possesses your mind, and like an addict you crave more and more attention. That's one of the reasons I felt that I should be on the floor with the microphone instead of Phil Donohue. I liked the attention so much I wanted to take over the program.

As expected, the demonstration flew by quickly. In television you never have enough time. Within a few scant seconds the couple had touched lips and the kiss was over. To my mind, with all those people watching and the prospect of millions of viewers in television land, there was no way this couple could enjoy the kiss. For a kiss to be enjoyable you need a certain degree of privacy, but there was absolutely no privacy here—just the opposite. Not only was everyone looking at them, but after the kiss was completed, Donahue began grilling them.

"How was it?"

"It felt good," the man said.

"But was it better than normal?"

"Um . . . yes."

Donahue turned to the woman.

"And what about you?"

"I liked it."

They were virtually speechless. But what could they say in such a situation? Everyone was counting on them to come up with something profound about how hypnosis had helped them enjoy the kiss. There's nothing about hypnosis in my book; instead, my message is all about enjoying the different types of romantic kisses with your partner. But I never got a chance to present this message on *Donahue*. Because of the way the producers had structured the segment, we had to go through this hypnosis stunt, adding a step that 99.99 percent of people will never experience. On the other hand, fully 100 percent of viewers will have tried a lip kiss, a french kiss, and most of the other kissing steps I write about in my books, so I felt that the producers should have let me talk for ten or fifteen minutes without interference. Again, there was my ego coming to the forefront, but that's how I felt.

Once you overcome your fear of public speaking and start enjoying the emotional rush of performing in front of an audience, the danger of developing an inflated sense of self becomes real enough to warrant careful consideration. I should have taken steps to reduce this danger, but I was a neophyte and I couldn't see that my ego was going to cause me numerous problems. So instead of dealing with this issue, I thrust myself right into the eye of the hurricane by seeking even more attention—the kind that could only do an egotist like me harm.

CHAPTER NINE

THE AMERICAN DREAM AND KISSING

PEOPLE WHO ARE ROMANTIC KNOW THAT there are generally two elements involved in a good kiss. First, it helps to have a connection with your partner—an emotional connection and a psychological attraction. Now, is it possible to dispense with this element? In other words, can you experience a terrific kiss with a total stranger? The answer to this question, according to my survey, is that, yes, it's *possible* to have a terrific kiss with a stranger, but only 2 percent of people said they had experienced such a kiss.

The second element involved in a good kiss is technique. Some people have a fine rapport with others and genuinely care for their partner, but they never achieve satisfactory kissing experiences—even with the one they love—simply because they're saddled with a kissing flaw, they make some basic mistake repeatedly, or they lack the fundamental kissing techniques that are a requirement for even minimal enjoyment.

The kissing show cannot help with the first element of a good kiss. In other words, we can't make two people fall in love. Nor can we provide the chemistry necessary between two people. Sparks either fly when you're together or they don't, and there's not much that anyone can do to fix that issue. Where the kissing show *can* help, however, is in teaching technique, something that a surprisingly large percentage of men and women lack, according to reports from their partners. In my survey, individuals aged thirteen to forty-six were asked, "How often do you have a partner who is lacking some element of kissing technique, such as kissing with too much saliva, choking you during a french kiss, or doing some other mechanical action that is off-putting or that ruins the experience for you?" About 45 percent of respondents felt that their partners suffered from technical problems. Interestingly, only 4 percent of women and 1 percent of men thought that *they* had technical problems themselves.

Once I compiled these statistics—and all the other data from the kissing questionnaire—I felt confident that I could offer something significant to young people at colleges across the United States. All I needed was the opportunity to get before these crowds, and I could help them by sharing the thirty different types of romantic kisses in my book. But how to get more gigs? There were, after all, only so many colleges in Boston, and even though it was a college town with more schools than most major American cities, I needed to spread my name and message farther across the country. In 1994, while I was mulling over how to get more gigs, a lucky coincidence sent me in the right direction. One of my acquaintances from my law school days happened to be Gina Eaton. She taught at Wheelock College and in her spare time lectured at other schools on the subject of violence against women. Gina and her husband were from England, and they had a young son. One day during a barbecue in her backyard I overheard her mention that she had a lecture agent and that she got paid to speak at colleges.

"Gina," I said. "Who's your agent?"

She looked up, surprised.

"Lordly and Dame, why?"

"Can I call them? I'm trying to get on the college lecture circuit."

"*You?*"

"Yes. I do a show at colleges."

"About what?"

"Kissing."

"*Kissing?*"

Suddenly everyone within earshot at the party was listening to our conversation.

"I direct a kissing demonstration based on my book."

Gina made a face that indicated she didn't think much of my topic.

"Nobody's going to represent a kissing show."

"Really?"

"Of course not. My show is about violence against women, and my presentation is based on research. It's academic. More than that, it fits in with many sociology courses, so schools are happy to bring me to their campus. But a *kissing* show? That's not something a booking agent would touch with a ten-foot pole."

I wasn't too happy with her answer. I knew for a fact that my show had drawn good audiences of enthusiastic students at every campus where I had presented it so far, and I felt it had a much wider potential. So a few weeks later when I ran into Gina at the apartment of one of our mutual friends, I brought up the subject again.

"Gina, listen," I began. "My show's working at local schools like Boston College, Babson, and Northeastern. Isn't there some way you could introduce me to your lecture agent?"

This time she had a more receptive attitude.

"My agents are too big, and they wouldn't consider a show like yours, especially since you've only done a few of them and your subject is so . . . unusual. But I used to work with a smaller agency. The owner's name is Kevin Moore, and he runs it with his wife, Jayne. They're young and aggressive. You might give Kevin a call."

With that promising lead, I called Kevin later in the week and introduced myself as a friend of Gina's. We talked for five minutes, and he said he would consider my show if I could send him some information about it.

"Do you have a video?" he asked.

That's something I hadn't thought to make.

"No, I don't."

"See if you can get one. Meanwhile send me your information."

I mailed my résumé a few days later, including a copy of my book, the flyers that Babson had put up to advertise my presentation, and a copy of the outline of my speech, together with a list of the shows I had done so far. Five months went by, and I heard nothing back from Kevin.

Although I was still good friends with Judy, I had started dating a girl named Arlene. One of the things I liked about her was that, like Judy, she had her own car and she was a good driver. But the thing about Arlene was that she was very ambitious, and she kept bugging me to give Kevin another call. When I got him on the phone again, I told him that I had an upcoming show at Stonehill

College in North Easton, Massachusetts. Kevin thought for a minute, and then he said he lived a short drive from the school and that if it was okay with me he'd come up and videotape the performance.

Even though she had her own car, Arlene and I got a ride to Stonehill from the organizer of the event. When we arrived at the school we started looking for Kevin, but he wasn't there yet. The presentation was scheduled in the college gym, and I completed a quick sound check. A hundred folding chairs had been set up close to the stage. I thought that should be sufficient because Stonehill was a small school. Then I started to rehearse my demonstrators backstage, though in this case backstage was simply a hallway at the side entrance to the gym. No one else was around and we had the space all to ourselves, which was perfect. Arlene sat beside me during rehearsal. One of the guys in the show was wearing a red sweatshirt, and he had blond hair and thick sensual lips. He was wearing glasses and looked like a rakish young scholar. His partner, a brunette with long hair, seemed to be having the time of her life during rehearsal. Before the show started, Arlene took me aside and spoke quietly to me.

"That guy in red is sexy."

"He is?"

"He looks at you, and just when you think it's getting to be too much, he looks away. And then he looks at you again—and you *feel* it!" She giggled, but I wasn't too happy that he'd been flirting with my girlfriend right in front of me. At any rate, I didn't let it bother me since this guy had his hands full with his demo partner, and it's always good to have demonstrators with sex appeal—an audience can sense that and it livens up the show. I started to wonder where Kevin was, but when I went into the venue and saw it overflowing with students I got distracted, and then the organizer of the event came up to me.

"Is this okay? We have over three hundred here."

"Sure!" I said. "The more the merrier."

There were so many students that most of them had to sit on the floor or stand in the back. While I was getting the audio assistant familiar with the sound cues, a thin fellow in his midthirties came up to me. He was wearing glasses and had jet-black hair, and he smiled warmly.

"Hi, I'm Kevin."

We shook hands.

"Great to meet you," I said.

"I've got my video camera set up over there." He pointed to the back of the room. "We can talk after the show."

A few minutes later I was introduced to a marvelously enthusiastic crowd. For me, this was bliss. They seemed interested in every quote from my book, and they laughed at every joke. Once the demonstrations started, beginning with the lip kiss, they went wild. In fact, this was the most electrified audience I had ever been fortunate enough to draw to my show. When it came time for the ear kiss, I stepped off the stage to allow everyone to focus on my four couples. Suddenly the crowd exploded into laughter, and I turned around to see what was making them scream. What I saw amazed me.

The boy in the red sweatshirt was stealing the show. Standing beside his partner with his hands in his pockets, he nonchalantly leaned forward to kiss the brunette's ears. The girl responded to that contact with a series of tremors that ran visibly through her body, and her excitement powerfully stimulated the audience. When the boy finally broke off, the brunette opened her mouth and gasped, fanning herself with one hand. The crowd screamed. When something magical like that happens, I like to step out of the way and allow the demonstrators to receive all the applause.

The rest of the show rolled along at the same high intensity and concluded on a positive note.

"It was great," Kevin said after it was over. "The students really loved it. I initially had some doubts about a kissing show, which is why Jayne and I never got back to you. But now that I've seen it and have a videotape proving that the show is a crowd pleaser, I'd be happy to represent you. Let's see if we can sell it to a few additional local schools, and then if that works, we'll reach out to a national audience."

My heart leaped. Those encouraging words from my new lecture agent promised to change my life. No longer would I receive a mere gift certificate to Pizzeria Uno's for directing the kissing show. Now I would command over $1,000 for a performance. Suddenly I faced the amazing prospect of earning more in two hours than I did in a whole semester of teaching. My life was going to change in many ways as a result of my association with Kevin and Jayne. Many good things were just over the horizon.

But so was my first paid gig.

CHAPTER TEN

THE UNIVERSITY OF NEW HAMPSHIRE

BEFORE I DESCRIBE THE FIRST GIG MY NEW lecture agents booked for me in 1995, I must make a little confession. Like many other firstborns I have a natural tendency to assume a leadership role whenever the opportunity presents itself. I grew up with a sister who was only a year younger, and two brothers who were two and a half and five and a half years younger. Without intending to be mean, but with an undeniable need to assert my firstborn inclination to rule the roost, I sometimes terrorized my siblings and ordered them about like a dictator. For example, one day I took a mirror off the wall and bounced beams of sunlight at them, yelling, "It's a Martian death ray! If it hits you it'll vaporize you on the spot. Don't let it touch you! Run for your life."

And run they did—maybe not believing they would *really* be killed—but caught up in the moment they ran, they screamed, and they were dutifully terrified.

This tendency I have to direct people, to order them about, and to guide them in various activities is something that has stayed with me from childhood into my adult years, and the good thing about this trait is how it helped me in the classroom, where I took to teaching like a duck to water. But while the positive side of this personality trait confers leadership ability, the negative side can turn into an annoying bossiness. Fortunately for everyone involved, during my first few gigs I managed to be all sweetness and consideration, leading my student demonstrators with abundant tact and civility. The bossiness problem didn't creep into the picture and become an issue until I had been directing the kissing show for six or seven years, as you'll see later. But for my first gigs, as a brand-new college speaker, I would need every ounce of that natural ability to lead.

When Kevin called me with the news of my first paid booking, I was elated.

"The University of New Hampshire saw your video and they liked it. I told them the price and they agreed. The school will also cover round-trip transportation from Boston and provide lodging for the night after the show at a local motel. Do you want to accept the offer?"

"Wow, Kevin! Are you serious? Of course I want to accept. This is exponentially better than getting a gift certificate to Pizzeria Uno's."

Kevin chuckled and assured me that from now on I would always be paid for my presentations.

"This is a lower amount than we're going to ask in the future," he said. "But because it'll be your first paid performance, we'll start low before we raise the fee. Some of our other speakers are regularly getting significantly more than this for a gig, and we may be able to bump your fee up into a higher range if things go well."

When I got off the phone I began pacing back and forth in my studio (yes, I was still living in that room in Brookline, Massachusetts). Going through my mind was one exciting thought: I was going to be paid over $1,000 for an hour's work, and to top it all off, it wasn't really work, was it? I mean, doing the kissing show was a blast—and most of all it was something that fed my ego like nothing else. And here I was going to get paid to do it. Unbelievable, truly unbelievable. I was grinning from ear to ear and I couldn't stop.

I was still grinning during my Amtrak ride from Boston to Durham, New Hampshire. When the student coordinator of the event picked me up at the station, I felt so filled with gratitude and enthusiasm that I could hardly believe my good luck. I kept pinching myself to see whether I was really awake. It was simply too good to be true—and yet it *was* true, and I was being driven to the venue, the school gymnasium, where I completed a quick sound check and then waited eagerly for my volunteers to show up.

You cannot understand my excitement unless you fully understand how easy doing the kissing show was for me. In terms of physical energy expended, it was admittedly a lot of work, since I spent forty-five minutes rehearsing with my volunteers and then immediately afterward I ran around the stage and through the audience as I directed the live performance. But although I would become physically exhausted after a show, it was not difficult work mentally. It was nothing like working in an office, and it was even easier and more fun than teaching. There was a similar dynamic to classroom teaching—which was always easy, even if I was tired—but the big difference, which made the show so much more fun for me, was that these students didn't feel roped into being there in the audience. Unlike students in a classroom, they could get up and leave without any penalty whenever they wanted. Over the course of directing the show for two decades, there were very few students who ever got up and left; they stayed because they wanted to stay. They sat there and gawked at the romantic interactions of the demonstrators, they screamed in excitement, and they usually gave every indication that they were thoroughly enjoying themselves.

And this is exactly the way that first show in New Hampshire went. It began with the audience of about three hundred listening attentively as I read some quotations about the first kiss from my book. I was carefully priming the audience for the big surprise that would come a few minutes later when I asked the couples to stand facing each other. As the crowd saw them leaning closer and closer for that first lip contact, they began screaming with pleasure and anticipation.

"*Yaaaaaaaaaaay!*"

"*He-he-he-he-he-he-he!*"

"*Ha-ha-ha-ha-ha-ha-ha!*"

And many cried: "*Oh my gaaaaaaaaaawd!*"

Folks, I kid you not, this is the riotous madness that greeted me when that first kiss occurred ten minutes into my first paid kissing show, and when they started screaming like that, what do you think I felt? Like any public performer, whether comedian, musician, or lecturer, a positive response like that rushes right through your nerves like the most powerful stimulant imaginable. Ask any performer and they'll tell you the same thing: it's a physical and mental high. You absorb energy directly from the audience, as if you were plugged into an electrical circuit, so that when they scream with joy, your nerves light up and their excitement zings right into your brain.

I was glowing with pleasure from that point on, especially since everyone seemed to love the show. Just like at Stonehill, where they had screamed and yelled when that fellow in the red sweatshirt kissed his partner, the UNH crowd screamed and laughed at all the demonstrations, none more than the car kiss at the conclusion of the performance. In that skit, I have the girls act as passengers and the guys as drivers; then the girls kiss the boys and the audience goes berserk and starts cheering. I closed the show the way I always did, with some additional quotations from my book, and a short question-and-answer period during which I replied to any questions from the audience that might have arisen during the demonstration.

I didn't realize it at the time, but after each performance my lecture agents had a policy of contacting the director of student activities, who was a staff person at the school, asking them two questions: How did the show go? And how did you like working with the performer?

Kevin called me a few days after I got home.

"I have some feedback from your first show at UNH. The director is a woman I've known for many years, and she's honest with me. She also knows that this was your first paid performance, and she thought it was a big hit with the students, so congratulations."

"Thank you."

"But she had one suggestion: she said that the car skit got an energetic response from the audience, but when you returned to read quotations from your book for five or six minutes and then took questions, the energy in the room died back down. She thought it would have more impact if you moved the quotations and the question-and-answer segment earlier and saved the exciting car skit for the finale."

I thought about this for a minute, but I was annoyed at the suggestion. Who was this woman to tell me how to organize and structure my material? I loved to read, and words mattered to me. I wanted people to appreciate my writing and all the research I had done in collecting those quotations. If I put the car skit last, that would detract from the literary quality of the show, diminishing my work and my role as an author, which I considered of paramount importance.

But I didn't say anything about this to Kevin.

"I understand where she's coming from," I said. "She thinks the show would have more impact with the car skit as the conclusion."

"To be fair," Kevin added, "I saw the show at Stonehill, and I have it on tape. You killed the audience there. I've hardly ever seen a college audience react that well to a presentation, but when you ended it by going back and reading from your book, the energy level died down, just like she's saying. You could see some students fidgeting."

"Okay, I'll rearrange things to put the quotations earlier," I said. "And I'll end with the car skit."

"Great, because I already have another school interested. They heard about the show, and I should find out within a week or two whether they want to book it."

When I got off the phone with Kevin, I started pacing again, letting off steam. I was still annoyed at that woman and Kevin for making the suggestion. But then I remembered that I was getting paid now, and I realized that I would have to take advice from my agent. I had full faith and confidence in Kevin Moore, and as time went on I began to think of him as an expert in the world of college performances. His advice, after all, wasn't intended to hurt me or detract in any way from my work as an author; on the contrary, he wanted the best for me, and if the show did well he would stand to make more commissions, just as I would stand to make more money from increased bookings. In the final analysis, he was squarely on my side. Once I arrived at that realization, I slowly but surely put aside my fear of losing primacy as an author. Nobody was downplaying my work—they were simply making an objective suggestion about how to structure the performance more effectively with a college crowd.

Over the next few days I made major changes to my outline. Initially I tried moving the quotations earlier in the show, but I already had plenty of quotes at the start, so I had to insert these other quotations into the middle of the performance. That didn't work either; it just interfered with the flow of the kissing demonstrations. Finally I tried eliminating some of the quotations and tightening the beginning of the performance at the same time. After making these edits, I wound up with about six or seven minutes of prefatory material before the demonstrations began, and now the show would conclude with the car kiss. I looked at my outline, sat back, and took a deep breath. There was no way to know whether this change would be successful until I tested it before a live audience, but I was eager to see what would happen when I attempted to implement the new arrangement.

To my surprise, I quickly had to admit that Kevin was, as usual, 100 percent right: after I made this adjustment, almost overnight word about the kissing show spread from school to school throughout New England, and it became the fastest-selling show on the college lecture circuit, booking so many gigs that I often had to direct two shows on the same day at different colleges. I wound up doing more presentations than ever, and I was grateful that I was learning the tricks of the trade from one of the most accomplished lecture agents in the business.

CHAPTER ELEVEN

THE RULES OF LOVE

THE MOST CELEBRATED WRITERS OF THE ancient world are nearly unanimous in their opinion that happy lovers achieve success by following a code of conduct called the Rules of Love. Ovid outlines these rules in a satirical manner in *The Art of Love*, Andreas Capellanus spells out similar rules in *The Art of Courtly Love*, and various other writers discuss these rules in stories about King Arthur and the Knights of the Round Table—one of the most delightful texts in this category having been written by an unknown author and entitled *The Quest of the Holy Grail.*

Even though I had doted on these books, I made the mistake of thinking that they were mere theoretical treatises or simple entertainment, and I ignored their time-tested advice. As a result I had to learn the rules of love the hard way, through trial and error.

The first blunder I made was one that my inflated ego forced me to commit. I'm sure you'll be amused to learn about this error because then you can be sure to avoid making it yourself, but I want to preface my recollection of this troublesome episode in my life by calling your attention to the fact that I'm by no means the only writer to have made this mistake. Many of my readers will be familiar with the work of Jack Kerouac, but I'll wager that few people know he kept a notebook in which he recorded the names of every girl he had intimate relations with, together with the dates of each of his amorous encounters. An entertaining summary of these liaisons appears in Ellis Amburn's *Subterranean Kerouac* (1998). Amazingly, Kerouac's little red book reveals that he had relationships with close to two hundred women. Admittedly, my diary contained exponentially fewer entries, but I made the same mistake the father of the Beat Generation made when I inadvertently allowed my paramours to look into my diary. While I was directing the kissing show I happened to be seeing two different girls at the same time. Naturally this required careful coordination on my part, especially since there were occasions when I was foolish enough to see both of them on the same day. Whenever I frolicked with these young women I would make a secret little notation in my diary. I'm not exactly sure *why* I kept such notes, but I confess that I do have an almost obsessive compulsion to record things; in fact, I even list what I eat and what exercises I do every day.

My girlfriends were curious women, and both of them knew that I kept a diary. On several occasions they each independently expressed a keen interest in reading it. Now when I reflect back on those halcyon days, I have a feeling that they may have had a suspicion that they would find something incriminating in my diary, but at the time the way they expressed their wish to read it was in completely innocent terms, such as, "I'd love to see what kind of creative ideas you jot down in your little book, my dear."

Or the equally seductive, "Would you mind terribly if I just took a peek into your private thoughts, honey? Pretty please?" Foolish me for falling for these entreaties! I have only myself to blame. You see, I was self-centered enough to think that they were really interested in my creative musings, and I was also confident that my secret notation symbols would be indecipherable. But my code was quite easy to break, and you didn't need to be a cryptologist to figure it out: all I did was place a little smiling face in my diary whenever I had an enjoyable little interlude with one of these inamoratas. Each page of my diary also happened to be printed with the hours of the day, so that my symbols were always placed next to the corresponding time when we had our romantic encounters.

Of course these women knew very well what day they saw me, and after they feigned interest in seeing my creative notations, they always turned immediately to the dates when they had been with me, curious to see whether I had written any notes or reflections about our assignations. Knowing, too, exactly what time of day they had been with me, they could plainly see that there was a smiling face at the precise hour when we had engaged in our romantic diversions. But on some of the diary pages there would mysteriously appear *another* smiling face— either earlier or later in the day . . . now, what could *that* mean? Why was there another smiling mark at eight thirty in the evening when we had been together at one in the afternoon? Inevitably the questions would arise: "Are you seeing another girl? . . . Tell me the truth: Do you have another girlfriend?"

I didn't realize it at the time, but one of the cardinal rules of love is that when suspected of having an affair, you need to refrain from hurting your partner, and according to those ancient codes, probably the best way to do this is by denying everything. In fact, Ovid spells this rule out explicitly in *The Art of Love*.

Though it's hard to say what to do in any situation as tricky as this one, in my case, I really should have followed Ovid's advice. When these young women found those smiling marks and grilled me about the possibility of my seeing another woman, I unwisely let my vanity get the better of me. I thought they would be impressed, but in each case they lashed out at me and made my life miserable. One of them eventually ended our affair. The other was annoyed for months, although we eventually got over it when I told her, truthfully, that I no longer saw the other girl and that I had never really been that deeply interested in her.

But the consequence of my violating this rule of love was that I was in a low frame of mind when I went on the road to do the show. My depression haunted me and took away from the vitality and effervescence that I would otherwise bring to my performances. So my strong advice is to keep your diary carefully hidden from your partners.

A closely related rule of love, and one that's directly applicable to anyone who is a public performer, is that you must never reveal to the audience or to the people who are hosting your presentation that you're heartbroken, disappointed in love, or so low in yourself that you're ready to break down and cry. Let me explain why this is an error by telling you what happened to me after I had been directing the show for several months.

When you travel to certain colleges that are in remote locations, you sometimes need to be picked up in a van where you'll be sharing a ride with a number of strangers. One day in the fall of 1997 I found myself in a crowded van with three men and a woman who were total strangers, and we were being driven to a location more than a hundred miles from the airport. They were going to be dropped off at various hotels, and I was going to be taken to my accommodations near the college where I would be speaking that evening. All I wanted to do during that drive was sit back and close my eyes and take a nap, but these people were very chatty and they wanted to pass the time by talking and sharing their life stories. I told myself to keep my mouth shut and tell them nothing. Whenever people find out that I wrote a book about kissing, they ask the same questions that I've heard a hundred times already: Why did you write a book about kissing? How did you do your research? How many girls have you kissed? What does your wife think about it? . . . and on it goes. Friends, at first these questions fueled my ego, but after you've heard the same inquiries ad nauseam, you prefer to hide your work from other people and remain anonymous. But I must have been in a weakened condition because two days before this trip a young woman I was pursuing had confessed that she had started dating one of the Kennedys. She had given me all the sordid details of their first date over the phone, and I was furious with her and annoyed with the world to the point where I desperately needed a little ego boost. So I talked with these people and admitted exactly why I was traveling to this out-of-the-way college. As expected, I became the center of interest for the remainder of the ride and they grilled me to death with all the old questions. But I had sunk into such a depressed mood that even their fawning attention couldn't dredge me out of my blue state—it only made it worse.

By the time I arrived at the campus I was feeling so low that when the young man who had organized the event took me into the cafeteria to buy me lunch, I broke the rule of love that says *keep your romantic woes to yourself and don't burden other people with them*. I told him all about my depressing little problem and explained that I was devastated. I didn't realize that heartache is something you need to keep to yourself as a performer for one simple reason: these people have paid thousands of dollars and invested their time and energy to bring you to their school, and they have a reasonable and legitimate expectation that you'll arrive in a state of mind where you're ready, willing, and able to give an effective performance. They are not your psychoanalyst, nor are they your confessor. They may act friendly, and you can be friendly with them, but you must not make the mistake of thinking that they care about your personal life. They are not the people to unburden yourself to; instead, tell a close friend or a trained therapist. Whatever you do, leave these people out of it. In fact, the less they know about your personal life, the better.

It ruined my working relationship to confess how down I was, and the poor young fellow, who was only nineteen, didn't know what to say. I should never have burdened him with my problems. More to the point, if I had said nothing to him—which was the correct approach to follow in this case—he would never in a million years have guessed that I was depressed. He didn't know me personally, and my demeanor isn't a dead giveaway. I have enough energy and experience to direct a show in a competent manner even when I'm not feeling my best, and I should have kept my mouth shut and done my job like a professional. It would have made this young man's life easier, and it certainly would have made it easier for us to work together.

Two days after I arrived home, Kevin called.

"You're probably not going to be invited back to that school."

"Why not?. . . Didn't they like the show?"

"The show was fine."

"Then what's the problem?"

"Don't you remember that I told you there are *two* things schools are looking for: one, a good show; and two, a person who's easy to work with."

"Wasn't I easy to work with?"

"The kid said you had psychological problems."

After that, whenever I was in a terrible mood I reminded myself how my lecture agent had helped me learn not only one of the most important rules for a public speaker, but also one of the most important rules of love: keep your mouth shut about your personal life—especially with total strangers, and especially with total strangers who have paid good money for you to speak at their school.

CHAPTER TWELVE

THE NAKED NECK

YOU CANNOT BEGIN TO IMAGINE HOW ridiculously hungry I was for media attention in the months immediately after my book was published. The best way I can explain it is to tell you about a curious incident that happened in the life of Arthur Schopenhauer. He published a beautifully written book in 1813 explaining why we can say that this or that thing or event has a cause, but we cannot say that the universe itself has a cause. The title of his treatise is *On the Fourfold Root of the Principle of Sufficient Reason*. In the course of this dissertation, he digresses momentarily to relate an anecdote about how he installed new curtains in his bedroom, and how his poodle, an intelligent little dog, sat staring up at them trying to figure out what caused them to open and close. Then Schopenhauer goes on to analyze his dog's mind and explain that even animals understand the concept of causation. Priceless, right?

Now, in the aftermath of the publication of *The Art of Kissing*, I was like Schopenhauer's dog: I would sit at home in my new apartment in Boston staring up at my curtains. And what was going through my mind? One simple question related to causation, repeated over and over almost every hour of every day: What will cause me to receive more publicity? When will I get the next phone call inviting me to be on television? When will a producer contact me and ask me to be on a national radio program? When will a big magazine or newspaper reporter request an interview about my book and my show? Virtually all my waking thoughts revolved around satisfying my narcissistic desire for more attention. In many ways it was like a sickness. I've already explained how I jumped at the chance to be in a television game show audience when I was a teenager, and how I leaped to my feet when the cameras panned across the spectators. The seeds of my mania had been planted early in life, and they were watered by every new television and radio show I did after my book came out in 1991.

So you can imagine my excitement when I received a call from *The Boston Globe* in the summer of 2000 requesting an interview. Not only that, but they wanted to send a reporter *and* a photographer to cover the story.

"We'd like to get a photograph of you kissing a girl," the newspaper woman said. "I can interview you later for the feature, but the photographer would like to come by tomorrow."

"Well, er . . . I, um—"

"Is there some problem?"

"My policy is that I don't personally demonstrate kisses for the media. I always have someone else do that."

"But this is different; it's a major feature story about you and your book. We'd really like to have a photo of *you* kissing your girlfriend."

Steam started coming out of my ears. I wasn't about to

admit to this reporter that I had recently had a tiff with the girl who was driving me crazy when she started dating one of the Kennedys.

"Listen, I'll tell you what," I said. "I can't get my girlfriend by tomorrow because she's away on a trip to Europe. But what if I get one of my students to stand in for her? I'll kiss *her* instead."

"That'll work."

Right after I got off the phone I called Jessica Beaton. She was in her midtwenties and was engaged, but she was one of my best friends. Now, the thing you have to understand about Jessica is that she possessed one of the sweetest dispositions you could ever imagine. Not only was she a sweet person, but she was also one of the most open-minded people I knew.

"What are you doing tomorrow?" I said.

"Nothing."

"I'll pay you $100 if you come over here and let me kiss your neck—"

"*What?*"

"It's for a *Globe* feature on my book."

"But what will Johnny think!"

"No, no, wait a minute—you don't understand—hold on a minute and let me explain, will you?"

"What's to explain? You'll get me in trouble with my fiancé. He's very jealous—"

"It's nothing like that. The *Boston Globe* is doing a feature story about my show, and they need to illustrate it with a photograph of me kissing some girl. As you know, I don't have a girlfriend right at the moment, so naturally I thought of you for this photo shoot."

Now she was laughing.

"Seriously, come on, can you do it? I swear I'll just kiss your neck for the photo. No tongue."

More giggling.

"But my boyfriend would kill me if I got my picture in the paper being kissed by you. He'll see it. He reads the *Globe* every morning."

"Okay, this is what we'll do. I'll tell the photographer to show nothing more than me kissing you on the neck, and to crop the photo so that your eyes aren't visible. This way no one will ever recognize you."

"Hmm—"

"But you'll still be a big shot with your friends because you can show them the paper and tell them it's *you*. Who knows, it might even lead to a modeling career." She *was* beautiful, but I knew she wasn't interested in modeling; still, flattery never hurts when you're trying to convince a girl to do something crazy.

"Let me think about it."

"What's there to think about? I need an answer right now. This photographer is coming over tomorrow at one o'clock. Come on, do it . . . please!"

Big pause—big sigh.

"Oh . . . okay."

The next day Jessica arrived wearing a gray sweater, which I thought would be good for the photo. But her hair was shoulder-length, which meant I would have to push it aside for the neck kiss.

"Do you want to rehearse?" I asked.

This provoked a sarcastic little chuckle and a mock frown.

"I don't need to rehearse getting kissed on the neck."

"Okay, have it your way. But when the photographer

gets here, let's be professional about the whole thing, okay? I'll explain that we don't want your boyfriend to recognize you, and that the newspaper needs to crop your eyes out of the shot."

"Be sure you do that."

I smiled at her, she smiled at me, and then we stood by my windows and gazed down at Boylston Street. I lived in a four-thousand-square-foot apartment with luxury amenities on the seventh floor of a nice building that I was able to afford only because of my earnings from the show.

"This is a nutty thing to do, isn't it?" Jessica said.

"Sure it is. But we're always doing crazy things. That's the way to live life to the fullest, don't you think?"

The bell rang and the photographer came in with his equipment. As expected, he had a busy schedule and there was no small talk. He unpacked his stuff, and within a couple of minutes he was ready to shoot.

"Listen, this is one of my students," I said. "She doesn't want to be identified by name in the caption or the story."

"No problem."

"And she doesn't want her boyfriend to recognize her. Is there some way you can crop her face out of the photo and just show me kissing her neck?"

"Let's see . . . I think we can do that. Why don't we have the girl stand in front of the window, facing us. And then you stand between the window and me, and kiss the side of her neck."

Jessica stood where instructed; she was one of the best actors I ever worked with as far as taking direction. She never complained, no matter what tasks she was expected to perform. Tell her to walk, she walked. Tell her to smile, she smiled. Tell her to arch her head back and receive a neck kiss, she arched her head back and waited to receive the neck kiss.

Click! Click! Click!

"Move a little to the right, Jessica."

Click! Click! Click!

"Cheat a bit toward me . . . chin up. Hold it!"

Click! Click! Click! Click! Click!

"I think I've got what I need. Thanks, guys!"

And then the photographer was gone. As soon as he was out the door Jessica started laughing, and so did I. We had accomplished a silly thing together.

"He better keep his word and crop the photo," Jessica said.

"Don't worry. I'm sure he will."

"When is it going to be published?"

"Tomorrow morning."

"Call me if you see it before I do."

"Okay."

I walked her to the door.

"And thanks, Jessica!"

The next day the photo appeared on page one of the *Globe*. As promised, it was a tight shot of me, my entire face leaning down to kiss a girl's neck—but thankfully you could *not* see the girl's face or eyes. Her head was turned away at a sharp angle, and all you could see was her pale clavicle and the lower part of her jaw. I was holding her hair back so it was hardly visible. The shot was in color, though, so you could tell I was kissing a brunette. But other than that, I thought we were safe.

I called Jessica right away to congratulate her. But what she said stunned me.

"I'm in trouble."

"*What?*"

"Johnny recognized me."

"How in god's name could he do that?"

"He's no idiot."

"But your eyes aren't visible."

"He knows that you wrote a book about kissing, and he knows that I know you, and that I'm always over there visiting you. He reads the paper every day. For crying out loud, there's my picture on the front page. Of course he saw it. And he's very intimately acquainted with my neck. You can clearly see the girl in the photo has dark-brown hair. He's been screaming at me all morning that I was getting kissed by you!"

"Didn't you tell him it was only your neck?"

"That doesn't matter. The fact that I was in your apartment alone with you and you were kissing me is the problem."

"I'm sorry."

Sure, I was sorry. But the truth is that both Jessica and I were smiling while we were talking about it, because it *was* a funny situation. Technically, we hadn't done anything wrong: she had simply provided her neck for a major newspaper story. Just like an actress will kiss an actor in a movie where there's no personal romantic connection, she had provided a stand-in neck for this photo, and her boyfriend didn't really have anything to worry about. But looking back with hindsight at what had happened between us, I can sympathize with his point of view. If the situation had been reversed, I would have been jealous as hell.

CHAPTER THIRTEEN

THE CAR KISS

YOUNG PEOPLE KNOW THE IMPORTANCE OF cars better than anyone. It's easy to see why, too, because automobiles play such an important role in the romantic life of most teenagers. Mustangs, Corvettes, and even old Buicks rescue boys and girls from the prying eyes of parents, whisking them away to beaches, parks, and hangouts where they can enjoy the privacy that Wilhelm Reich asserted is the birthright of young lovers everywhere.

You can listen to music in cars, kiss in cars, and most important of all, you can show off in cars: other people will see you and get jealous.

I had included the car kiss from the beginning of the show, but as I've already explained, the car kiss evolved over time: the first iteration occurred ten minutes prior to the conclusion of the program, and then at the suggestion of my agent, I moved it to the end of the show. But my overactive imagination didn't rest with this highly effective modification, even though it supercharged the event with an exciting and memorable finale. In fact, in 1996 I set out to do additional research to see if I could make a good thing better.

At the time, I was going out with Judy Youngson, a girl I had met at a feminist meeting in Cambridge during my law school days. She had straight black hair and a very kissable mouth. There was always something ironic in her smile, and I never got tired of trying out new kisses with her. Luckily she had a car and was a good driver too. My eyesight had deteriorated over the years, and as a result I let her do all the driving, and by this I mean I never took the wheel of her car, not even once. Instead I would sit beside her and enjoy being chauffeured here and there by this charming young woman. She was relaxed and easygoing, especially since we were completely crazy about one another. All I had to do was glance over at her and I would start thinking about various kisses I would like to try.

This kind of romantic situation is the ideal setup for creative thoughts. It gives you the peace of mind you need for dreaming up new ideas and devising inventive ways to kiss.

One summer we took a vacation together and she rented a cabin in New Hampshire. I had no cares or responsibilities, and there were no shows on my schedule. In the afternoon we went swimming in Lake Winnipesaukee, and at night we ordered pizza delivered to our cabin. Sometimes we took walks along the beach. It was during this time of extended leisure that my mind dreamed up a new idea to try in the car skit. The idea came to me at twilight while we were sitting in the backyard of the cabin barbecuing dinner. Judy was standing in front of the grill cooking the food, and I was sitting in a lawn chair about five or six feet away. All of a sudden, maybe because I was looking at the way we were positioned, it occurred to me that if I rearranged the chairs in the show at a right angle to the audience—instead of directly facing the crowd—I could heighten the resemblance to driving on a highway. I was so excited by the idea that I sprang up and took Judy by the shoulders.

"Drop that spatula."

"Why?"

"Because I want you to sit down."

I turned her chair away from the grill so that it was facing the cabin. I moved my chair next to hers. Then I stepped back. She was staring at me as if I had lost my mind.

"But the burgers are going to burn—"

"Don't worry about that."

She humored me and sat patiently waiting. I stepped back another few feet to survey the scene.

"Put your arms up as if you're driving."

She did as instructed.

All of a sudden I could see it clear as day: the demonstrators would be sitting facing to the right, just as Judy was now. I would instruct the boys to pretend they were driving. The audience would see a realistic simulation of four couples speeding down the highway. Then the skit would escalate the romantic tension as the girls began kissing the guys in the moving car. With this new arrangement it would be a hundred times more effective.

All at once, black smoke billowed up from the grill and Judy jumped out of her chair. The hamburgers were well-done that night, but the car skit was mightily improved. I became so excited that when I got inside I drew a picture of the way I wanted it to look: I had three couples, all facing sideways to the audience, and the girls would be in the back—that is, upstage of the boys. This way the audience would have to struggle a little to see them, which would enhance interest since the girls would be doing the sexy stuff at the beginning of the scenario—kissing the boys on the cheek, then on the mouth, and then once again on the mouth as they climbed up on their partner's lap.

When I returned to the lecture circuit in September I immediately introduced these modifications into the car skit. Now the show not only closed with the most exciting scenario, but the way it was staged contributed much more punch to the conclusion. At the same time, I added Chuck Berry's "No Particular Place to Go" as the soundtrack for the skit, and I timed my remarks to coincide with the cadence of the song. The rhythmic nature of the way I belted out my commands to the demonstrators added to the effectiveness of the scene.

The car skit followed the penultimate scenario, called the Trobriand Islands kiss, which occurs on a South Pacific island in a grass hut. I would always signal the transition into the car scenario with the line "But we don't need grass huts . . . because we're in America!"

These words were the cue to my sound engineer to start the music track.

The demonstrators were listening to me for their cues, and I always delivered the next line in a raised voice so that they would jump into position:

"They're in their cars, their chairs facing to the right, and the boys are driving." The first few times I said this, the audience laughed. I was puzzled until I realized that I had set things up with the boys sitting on the right-hand side of the car. But I needed it that way to make the girls appear more mysterious and harder to see. So I added the line, "Yes, they're in London." This line truly made no sense because I had started the skit by saying, "We don't need grass huts . . . because we're in *America*." But I wasn't concerned with making sense. Yes, we started in America, then we were in London—it didn't matter. The point was they were loving couples, they were in a car, they were driving together, and that's all you needed to get a college audience excited. I continued belting out the lines in sync with the music:

"He's driving fast—and she kisses him on the *cheek*."

If I had rehearsed them properly, my demonstrators would time their actions perfectly and the boys would have their hands up as if holding a steering wheel. In early run-throughs, though, the boys invariably turned their heads and bodies toward the girls and hugged and kissed them too soon. This destroyed the pace of the skit. I needed things to escalate as I had envisioned in New Hampshire. So I introduced the line: "He's got his hands on the wheel, his eyes looking straight ahead—*not* at the girl—as he drives at speed, foot pumping the accelerator." This instruction gave the guys additional actions to perform so that they were distracted enough not to look at the girls, which is exactly what I wanted.

Next I said, "She kisses him on the *mouth*."

All four girls did this at precisely the same time, and from the audience's perspective it looked beautifully choreographed. But to prevent the boys from disturbing the scenario, I had to add the line: "He turns up the radio to impress her." Again this line gave the boys additional stage business so that they didn't make the mistake of turning to the girls and hugging and kissing them again, which I wanted to save for the finale. The line also served as a sound cue for my engineer to raise the volume as we approached the conclusion of the skit—and of the show. Then I barked out my next instruction:

"She puts her *left* leg over *his* left leg . . . and kisses him on the mouth!"

I had to specify *which* leg because when I started doing this skit, the girls always took the easy way out and hooked their right leg over the guy's left leg, which looked tepid. But when I changed the instruction to tell the girls to put their *left* leg over his, they needed to get half off their seat to do it. The audience could not believe their eyes—here comes this car barreling down the highway at full speed *and the girl is climbing onto the boy's lap to kiss him*!

Then I issued my final instruction:

"He raises one hand off the wheel . . . and begins to *spank* her."

The boys had been carefully rehearsed to ensure that they raised their hands up to high heaven in order to give the audience something sensational to anticipate, and then they brought their hands swiftly down onto the backsides of the girls, who were still straddling the guys. Music blared from the speakers and filled the hall, and the audience went into paroxysms of screaming and laughing. All I had to do was deliver the closing line to bring down the house:

"And this is American kissing—at its best!"

CHAPTER FOURTEEN

THE STUPIDEST THING I EVER DID

THE GIRL BEHIND THE WHEEL WAS LOOKING better than ever, but that may have been because I had swallowed sixteen dexies with a can of beer before we got into her car. Yes, she was driving *me*, I was her passenger, and I was feeling pretty good about the whole arrangement.

It had taken me a few months to come to the conclusion that I needed to try something new in order to shake up my normal routine. It was 1998 and I had already directed scores of performances of the kissing show while perfectly sober. Then one day it occurred to me that maybe I should try to direct one of these shows in a state other than complete sobriety. After giving this plan some thought I decided that alcohol wasn't the best mind-altering substance to use because I needed to have my wits about me during the rehearsal and performance, so I only consumed one beer, which would be largely cleared from my system by the time I got to the school. I was going to rely on Dexedrine for this event.

Within minutes the pills were churning up my insides. I wondered if I had taken too many. The most I had ever taken before was five, and that had kept me up for two days. But this time I had more than tripled the dose. I figured what the heck, I didn't have to sleep for a week afterward anyway. On this occasion I was going down to Providence to direct a kissing show at a small college. The driver was my former student Cathy Antonopoulos. She had driven me to numerous local schools over the past couple of years, and in order to save on rentals I had given her $2,000 to buy the car we were using.

I wanted to be in a terrific mood the whole time I was doing this gig. The fact is, I *was* in a terrific mood when I got into the car. But sitting in the plush red passenger seat I felt I was on a roller coaster instead of in an Oldsmobile Cutlass Ciera. Every time we went over the slightest bump I could feel the shock waves vibrate through my spine. With each second that ticked by, the jolting sensations grew stronger and sharper.

Cathy kept leaning over to change the station on the radio. Every time she did her blonde hair fell to the side, obstructing her view of the road. She was very particular about the music. All she needed to hear was a fraction of a second of any song to know it wasn't right for her. *Click!* She switched to another station. *La—la—Click!* Another station . . . *La—de—da—Click!* Another! No good! Another! *Clickety-click, yakedy-yak, blah, blah, blah! Click! click! click! click!*

This nonsense was driving me insane. It never stopped. No song was good enough for her. And now the car was swerving in its lane. It was a gray afternoon, threatening rain. Luckily there weren't that many other cars on the road, but still it was a nail-biting experience to be sitting there with her holding the wheel with one hand, not even looking out the windshield, her eyes glued on the radio.

Click! . . . Another station . . . *click! click! click!*

Keep your eyes on the road, I'm thinking. *Keep your eyes on the road, will you! I paid you to drive me to this school—can't you at least keep your eyes on the road and do your job!*

Beads of sweat popped up on my brow. My stomach had twisted into a knot.

Without warning she pulled into a gas station, swerving and narrowly missing an oncoming van. Then she got out to go to the bathroom while the attendant filled the gas tank. As I waited for her to come back I started to get sick to my stomach. It was the amphetamines making my nerves twitch. My right foot kept jerking up and down uncontrollably. I slapped my hand down on my knee. I had to stop it before I got to the school or they'd see there was something wrong with me.

Cathy returned with a package of Hostess Sno Balls. Once we were back on the road she ripped the cellophane with her teeth.

"D'you want one?"

"No, thanks."

"They're good."

"I don't think my stomach could handle it."

"You might need some energy for the show."

"It's not that. I need to calm my stomach."

"You're not sick, are you?"

"No," I lied.

She started eating the cake, holding it in her right hand, driving with the left.

"Change the channel, will you?"

I leaned forward and switched to a new song.

"No good."

I changed it again.

"I don't like this one."

I changed it again.

"I'll do it. Here, can you hold this?"

She passed me the Sno Ball. Then she started switching channels again. I could feel the coconut with uncanny clarity. Every nerve in my hand was firing at ten times its normal intensity.

"Go ahead, take a bite."

"No, I can't."

She finally hit on an acceptable song, and she took the cake from me and polished it off. Meanwhile her driving had deteriorated to the point where I was considering asking her to stop the car. I had a splitting headache, too, but I wasn't sure my judgment of her driving skills was accurate. Maybe I was just suffering from paranoia caused by my heightened senses. I held my tongue and decided to be a man and risk getting killed.

We arrived on the campus of Rhode Island College. It was all manicured lawns, Colonial Revival architecture, and neofuturistic structures with monstrous green-tinted windows. When we walked into the venue, a small gymnasium, it was deserted. There was no stage either. Two hundred empty chairs gave mute testimony to the school's complete lack of preparation.

The director of student activities, a tall woman in her thirties, arrived with a clipboard.

"We couldn't get any volunteers."

This was the worst possible news. The whole thing depended on my having an opportunity to rehearse the demonstrators beforehand. Otherwise, anyone who volunteered at the last minute wouldn't know what to do. Unrehearsed demonstrators were a nightmare to work with, except in those rare instances when they were spontaneous. They usually got embarrassed and gave me a lot of flak about doing any of the unusual kisses, especially the spanking kiss, the Trobriand Islands kiss, and the car kiss at the end of the show. The whole effect could be ruined when I had to take people out of the audience and thrust them up in front of everyone without rehearsal.

But that's what I was faced with here. By the time the show was scheduled to start, only nine kids had straggled into the gym. It was an embarrassment. I had wanted to impress this little college with how sophisticated the show was so that maybe other schools in the area would book me to direct performances, but you couldn't do that with just nine people. For the love of heavens, I had done many shows with more than nine people *onstage*. Now I was faced with the difficult task of saving a hopeless situation. Meanwhile, my stomach was doing flip-flops from the dexies, and my hands were trembling so much I couldn't hold the microphone. I put it down. I didn't need a microphone anyway. I used my best manners and finally coaxed three kids to be demonstrators, two boys and one girl. The odd boy out sat alone at the edge of the performance area. The couple looked at me with anxiety written on their faces. *What had they gotten themselves into!* I could see their concern, so I tried to reassure them.

"Don't worry, this is going to be easy."

The girl was pale as a ghost, and her partner looked like a deer caught in headlights. There was nothing more I could do for them. I turned to the remaining six people in the audience. "This is a cozy group." I had to make them feel okay. It's always more difficult to go to an event when there are so few people in the audience because you feel that the speaker is depending on *you* to pay attention. And who knows, he might even call on you to participate. "I'm not going to call on any of you *unless you're sitting in the back.*" The four kids in the back looked around uneasily. Now they were at risk of being called upon. "Come on, move up, and I won't call on you." First one, then another, and finally all four moved up to the first two rows. This was exactly what I wanted, keeping it tight and cozy, a much more controllable experience for me.

I had asked Cathy to videotape the performance. She was in the back of the group with my camcorder, moving left and right in a totally amateurish way. I had a feeling that the video would turn out horrible, but I had more important problems to worry about.

Uppermost in my mind was something my agent Kevin had once told me. Despite the small turnout I was still going to get paid, *but only if I managed to finish the show without insulting anyone or causing the whole thing to fall apart.* So I commanded myself to get my act together and be extra nice to everyone so that they would all remain in their seats for the fifty-five-minute performance. The boy who was alone was supposed to be waiting for a girl to volunteer from the audience to join him. I asked if any of the girls would like to get into the act. But the girls in the audience looked frightened, and eventually I realized it was useless.

"You can go back to your seat," I told him. "I'm sorry we didn't get you a partner." He looked relieved.

Now I was faced with the dismal prospect doing a

show with only one couple when the minimum I needed was three. I had to make the best of the situation, so without further ado I launched into the show proper. I pushed myself to get through the preliminary remarks, which ordinarily consisted of seven or eight minutes of jokes and readings from my book. I wanted to get to the heart of the performance to keep everyone interested, and that meant getting the couple to kiss. They had told me that they were just friends, so I was worried that they might be shy about kissing—and, boy, was I right. They couldn't do it!

When I got to the first kiss, which was supposed to be no more than a light touching of the lips, they looked at me like I was crazy.

My heart was hammering in my chest. I could see every little wrinkle of concern rippling across their faces. I turned to them, my back to the audience, and addressed them in a friendly manner.

"Listen, this is a kissing show. But it's going to be easy. You don't even have to use any tongue. This is a simple first lip contact. All you do is touch your lips together."

They were still looking at me like I was out of my mind. They weren't even interacting with each other. The whole thing was falling apart.

"Okay, okay, listen." I was struggling to keep the desperation out of my voice. "Don't look at *me*. Turn your head toward *your partner*. That's it. Now lean closer and closer . . . and I'll talk you through the whole thing. Closer, baby, closer!" During a typical show, where I would have maybe three hundred people in the house, this was the moment when screaming and howling would commence, combined with nervous and excited laughter. But here the entire room was silent as a church. No one seemed to be having a good time. I had to lighten the mood or we would come to a crashing halt, but most of all I had to get them to do this first lip contact or it would all go downhill from here. I mean, if they couldn't do a simple *lip kiss*, what would happen when I tried to get them to do a biting kiss, a sliding kiss, or, heaven help us, lip-o-suction?

I stepped right up to them and began talking sotto voce, coaxing them as gently as possible. They moved close enough to kiss, but then they leaned their heads away from each other. Their shoulders were almost touching but their heads had arched too far back. As a last resort I whispered, "You can do it." The girl was a short brunette with long hair, and the guy was stocky, with almost a crew cut. I kept talking gently to them, hoping they wouldn't get spooked by the fact that I was so close.

Finally it happened—*lip contact*!

Although they touched lips for no more than a second, I could feel a wave of relief surge through the small group. We had achieved a milestone. This kiss was usually easy at other schools, but here it had been torture. At least it was over.

The rest of the show proceeded in a similar manner. I had to coax them through every little kissing scenario. They failed to do a good job with the more difficult maneuvers, like lip-o-suction, the biting kiss, and the Trobriand Islands kiss. But by the time we reached the finale they were following my directions, and they did a respectable job with the car kiss, the girl putting her leg over the boy's leg while he pretended to drive. She kissed him, music blared from the loudspeakers, and we received a smattering of applause to close the show.

By this time I was drenched with sweat. How I had managed to hold it together through the entire performance I'll never know. I thanked the demonstrators, packed my props, and collected my check from the director of student activities. On the face of it the check said, "Pay $2,500" to my lecture agents. *Amazing, right?* What a relief! All that money for an hour of work. But in this case it really *had* been work, and I had been forced to use all my tact and experience to make it succeed for this school.

Cathy and I headed back to the car.

"It's too bad there were so few kids present," she said.

We didn't want to talk about it in front of them, of course, but it was the topic of conversation as she began driving me home. It was dark and drizzling as we merged onto the highway. And that's when I made my mistake.

Cathy turned to me and said, "Professor, do you know how to drive?"

This is where I should have said something sensible like, "Yes, I know how to drive, but I'm not the best driver in the world."

Instead, the dexies were making me feel like Superman and I thought I could do anything. So I said, "Sure, I know how to drive."

That was the beginning of the end.

"I'm tired," she said.

I looked at her.

"I can hardly keep my eyes open."

She was supposed to be my driver. That's why I was paying her $355. Drive me to the event and drive me home. That's all she had to do. At least she could have had the presence of mind to drink some coffee or take amphetamines to keep herself awake for the drive. Instead, she was copping out on me.

"Can you drive?" she asked.

I couldn't believe my ears.

But in my drugged condition it seemed to me that I *could* drive the car. The last time I had gotten behind the wheel I had almost killed myself, I was so stressed out by the challenge of making my way through Boston traffic. Incredible as it was, even though I knew I was a terrible driver, not to mention amped up on dexies, I interpreted this situation as one I could handle without any problem.

"Of course I can drive."

"Are you sure?"

"Yes. I have a license."

I didn't tell her it was a license to kill.

"Okay, I'll stop here."

She pulled over to the side of the highway, and we got out and changed places. I settled myself behind the wheel.

I looked at the controls in some bewilderment. She must have noticed my confusion.

"Take it out of park."

She was giving me orders, but that didn't bother me because I needed direction. I had forgotten everything I knew about how to drive.

I should explain a curious aspect of Cathy's personality here. She loved to have a man take charge of things. Ironically, even though she should have sensed how dangerous it was for me to drive, she ignored this fact and seemed to drift into a fantasy world where the guy would save the day by taking the wheel. I was amazed how she continued to give me guidance on how to control the car, as if the man should *always* be in control even if he was an incompetent driver like me.

"Put it in gear."

I shifted into first.

"Step on the gas and steer onto the road."

I stepped on the accelerator, and we began to move.

"Check the side-view mirror to make sure the lane is clear."

I did as instructed. Friends, if you had been there to see this scene you would have been laughing at me, just as I'm laughing as I remember it and write it down for you. Before long, there I was, hands gripping the wheel, driving through a drizzle down a rain-soaked highway in the dark. I was going thirty miles an hour to be safe. The posted speed limit was fifty-five. Other cars were whizzing past.

"Go a little faster," Cathy said.

I increased our speed. I brought it up to forty-five, then fifty-five, trying to see how fast I could go without crashing. For some reason I started thinking about Albert Camus. Hadn't he killed himself in a car accident?

"Good," Cathy said. "You're doing good."

I felt elated at this kind word. It confirmed the inflated opinion I had of my driving skills. I was doing her a big favor since I was paying her to drive, yet here I was driving *her*. But then she said something that disturbed me.

"Do you mind if I close my eyes and take a nap?"

I turned to her. She was going to take a nap! Now I wouldn't have another pair of eyes on the road. I would be totally on my own.

"Sure, go ahead."

She closed her eyes, and I continued to drive. The car

was moving erratically down the highway and I was getting the jitters because I couldn't keep it from veering out of my lane. She had purchased such a cheap car that there was too much play in the steering gear. To make matters worse, the rain had picked up, and I couldn't see out the windshield.

Cathy blinked open her eyes.

"I'm sorry, my windshield wipers aren't the best."

Every few seconds the wipers would clear a small swath for me to peer out and get my bearings, after which I was totally blinded by water again. *How in God's name was I supposed to get us safely home?* I had no idea, but I was too hyped up on Dexedrine to back down.

After a few minutes Cathy opened her eyes again, just as we approached a toll booth.

"We have to pay the toll."

"Don't worry," I said. "I'll pay it."

"You have change?"

"Of course."

I approached the toll booth and saw that I wasn't going to be able to reach the basket where you deposit the coins unless I got the car over some more. So I turned the wheel to the left and inched forward until I was close. I stepped on the brake and the car shuddered to a halt. Cathy had her eyes closed again. I fished a few quarters from my pocket, dropped them into the basket, and waited for the green light . . . *Bingo!* The arm in front of us went up, giving the go-ahead to proceed.

I stepped on the gas.

But I had neglected to straighten the wheel.

In response to my pressing the accelerator the Olds leaped forward and crashed into the wall of the toll booth.

The sickening *Crunnnnnnnch!* of metal grating on

concrete seemed to echo and reverberate forever. The car lurched to a dead stop.

The next thing I knew Cathy was wide-awake and screaming.

"What did you do!"

I couldn't say a word. I was in shock.

"You crashed my car! . . . You crashed my car!"

I didn't want to annoy her further by reminding her that I had paid for the car. Technically it was my car since I had paid for it, but she kept yelling that I had crashed *her* car.

She got out and walked around to look at the bumper. There was a frown on her face.

"It's smashed in," she announced.

I got out to look. An accordion-like dent had crumpled the left fender, and the side of the car was severely damaged.

Cathy got back into the driver's seat. I went around to the passenger side and got in. She began to drive in silence.

"Don't worry," I said. "I'll pay for the repair."

No reply.

She didn't talk to me for thirty minutes. I was feeling disheartened about the whole incident, but eventually Cathy got over the shock of seeing the car dented and I guess she saw the humor in the situation because she started smiling. Before long the two of us were driving back in the rain laughing like maniacs. I vowed then and there never to use Dexedrine again while doing a gig. It was probably the stupidest thing I ever did—but in a way it brought us closer to have gone through that harrowing night together.

Our next little adventure would take us to Nashville.

CHAPTER FIFTEEN

THE NACA CIRCUS

HAVING INVESTED YOUR TIME PERUSING this book, you certainly deserve take-home value and in this chapter you're going to receive it with several unbeatable pieces of advice that I know for a fact you can't find anywhere else. Let's begin by picking up our story right where we left off last chapter, with me returning from a bomb of a show in Connecticut where only nine students showed up.

It may sound strange, but I wasn't depressed about what had happened. After all, it was the school's own fault for failing to do the advance work to publicize an event that they were paying thousands of dollars to bring to their campus. What they should have done was put up posters, made announcements in various classes, and in every other way possible spread the word like other colleges did. Even my lecture agents weren't worried about what had happened.

"Just remember to encourage the student running the event to publicize it," Jayne told me. "It's their responsibility, but it doesn't hurt to remind them of a few things they can do, like sending a mass email to their campus, for instance."

"Sure, Jayne, I'll do that next time."

"Hold on. Kevin wants to talk with you."

I thought Kevin was going to chew me out, but when he got on the phone he wasn't angry at all; in fact, what he said totally surprised me.

"Billy, the NACA regional convention is coming up and we'd like to submit the kissing show."

"Hunh?"

"Don't you know what NACA is?"

"No."

"It's the National Association for Campus Activities. They help schools decide which acts to book, so it's great publicity. They've got seven or eight conferences every year around the country. These conferences are huge three-day events with a lot of different booths for students and advisers to check out."

"Do you and Jayne have a booth?"

"Of course we do. And we want to submit *The Art of Kissing* for consideration to be in a showcase. By the way, a showcase is a short version of your presentation. It's limited to twenty minutes. If you're selected to perform at the conference, hundreds of students and advisers will get to see a preview of your show."

"Hmm."

I didn't react too enthusiastically, since the whole idea sounded pointless to me. It seemed to involve a lot of work and I didn't want to do it. I already had a full touring schedule, but my biggest objection was that I didn't understand exactly what this NACA showcase entailed.

"The fee for entering the selection competition is $200, and if you're selected the cost is $600, plus you'll have to fly down to the conference city and stay in a hotel for two or three nights. Your total out-of-pocket expenses will come to around $1,000."

Now I *really* didn't want to do it.

"Sure," I lied. "I'd love to do it."

"Great! Well, then I'd like to fly to Boston to go over the showcase with you. What you need to do is edit your program down to twenty minutes. Be sure to select only the most exciting kisses. Cut your introduction to half a minute, and then jump right into the demonstrations."

"But who's going to *do* the demonstrations? We're not going to be at a school, are we?"

"Hundreds of students will attend the convention. Maybe you can ask some of them."

After I got off the phone I started pacing up and down in my room. While I wasn't too upset about the bombed show in Connecticut, I was feeling generally overworked with the stress of so many shows. Crazy as it may sound, I was hoping that Kevin and Jayne would find a new act to represent, which would take some of the burden off my shoulders. Jayne had started answering the phone, "The Kissing Agency!" and she even told me that they had bought a new house as a result of the income my show generated. And now I was getting myself into this new venture. Why, oh why, did I agree to this madness? I reviewed my life up to this point: all I had wanted to do was write a book, and then the book attracted media, and then college students began asking me to talk about the book. Before I knew it I had a lecture agent and I was traveling from state to state doing shows, often staying away from home for weeks at a time. And now I was being roped into this complicated and expensive showcase thing. What in God's name was it, anyway?

I tried to calm my nerves, but I felt that my life was careening out of control. I had simply wanted to be a writer, someone sedate and composed, perhaps a little intellectual, like good old Erasmus, enjoying a quiet monkish existence, without any undue distractions or hoopla, but now—but now—

For pity's sake, but now I had a week to prepare *a showcase*? Kevin had explained it, but I was still unsure exactly what it meant. He said it needed to be only twenty minutes long, but in my opinion that was an affront to my intelligence. I had spent months perfecting my show, and it worked like clockwork. I had all my jokes carefully timed, I had all my segues from kiss to kiss mapped out, and I knew where to walk, what to say, and how to direct my student demonstrators. Now all of that needed to be truncated into this abbreviated format.

It annoyed me to realize that I had agreed to cut my performance so severely . . . and all because Kevin had some harebrained scheme to get us more gigs. Why was I risking my time and my money—$1,000!—to participate in this risky venture?

Friends, the lesson I learned the hard way is that a job is a prison, and my job was doing a kissing show. Sure, I taught English at Boston College, but the salary I earned was nothing compared with the kissing show: in seven hours I could earn more than I'd make in an entire year teaching. So my real job, let's face it, was the kissing show, and now this wonderful show that I thought had liberated me from teaching, this *job* was taking over my life. It had its shackles around me and I was a prisoner. When you stop and think about it, these showcase requirements were coming from hundreds of thousands of college students—

they were the ones driving the NACA organization, and it was ultimately these students who were making Kevin fly out from Wisconsin, where he now lived, back to Boston to help me rehearse the showcase.

I spent hours working on my outline to pare it down to twenty minutes. I selected the most exciting skits, including the first kiss, the vacuum kiss, the upside-down kiss, and the car kiss. When Kevin arrived a week later he sat in front of my desk and asked me to run through the showcase for him, word for word, indicating where the demonstrations would take place. And, friends, wouldn't you know it, he took out a stopwatch.

You have to understand that my father was a counseling psychologist and his specialty was testing, so when I was a kid he did all kinds of tests on me. He gave me IQ tests, inkblot tests, thematic apperception tests, Strong-Campbell interest inventories—and probably some more I don't remember. One day when I was seven he locked me in the kitchen and took out a velvet case, which he unzipped, and from which he carefully removed six beautiful wooden blocks painted with red diagonal lines. "You will arrange the blocks so that the red lines are touching," he said. "You have thirty seconds. Begin!" *Then he clicked the stopwatch.* After the time was up, he returned the blocks to the velvet case, zipped it up, and I never saw them again.

To this day I get heart palpitations whenever I'm faced with a timed test.

"Do you have to use that stopwatch?" I said.

Kevin looked up at me like I was crazy.

"They're going to have a stopwatch on stage in front of you, a big red countdown timer. So you better get used to doing this showcase in twenty minutes because they don't let you go overtime."

I started sweating.

"Okay," I said. "Start the clock."

Kevin clicked the stopwatch—and I was off! For twenty minutes he quietly sat there and listened.

"Time's up!"

I still had the end of the Trobriand Islands skit and the entire car skit to do.

Kevin shook his head and frowned. "You went over time. You're going to have to cut one of the kisses."

We worked all afternoon, and I rehearsed the showcase about five or six times until I could do the entire thing in under twenty minutes. Kevin advised me to leave a little leeway for unpredictable mistakes that might happen under the pressure of a live performance. When he left, I still didn't know what a showcase was.

I confess that I had many fears about going to my first NACA convention, so I decided to ask Cathy to accompany me. This was supposed to be a convention of college students, and she was a college student, so maybe she could help me cope with it. She didn't know what a NACA convention was either, but when I told her that I would pay for her airfare to Nashville as well as for her private room in a five-star hotel, she was raring to go.

Here's where I learned another life lesson from having to do a showcase, and it's one I had to figure out myself. The college had all sorts of rules against fraternizing with your students, but I felt that bringing Cathy along was within the limits of those rules, even if pushing them slightly. Sometimes it's necessary to push rules to their limits in order to accomplish a worthwhile goal. In this case, I was traveling to Nashville with one of my former students who I expected would help me deal with the uncertainty of this important convention. Not only had Cathy assisted by driving me to local gigs, she had also listened to me discuss the challenges of interacting with people at these schools. Having her along was like traveling with my own personal psychotherapist. The funny thing is that although Cathy seemed excited by the experience, she also appeared closed to some of the fun of the trip. When we took off from Logan airport she was sitting by the window, and I was in the middle seat.

"Look, there's Boston College," I said, pointing out the window.

"No, it's not," she said.

"Yes, it is. We're flying directly over the building where we had our English class, McGuinn Hall."

"Not true."

Hunh? I was thinking. *Is she blind?* Then for the rest of the flight she didn't even look out the window.

Despite how oblivious Cathy acted regarding her surroundings and how she sometimes exhibited quirky and bossy personality traits, I really liked her—maybe because she reminded me a little of myself. Underneath her brusque exterior she possessed an endearing, almost childlike vulnerability. It rarely came to the fore, but when it did it was irresistible. For instance, she once said, "Professor, don't hold it against me. I'm like this with everyone. I can't help it." I mean, how could you not be won over by such a confession?

When we arrived in Nashville we took a taxi to the Gaylord Opryland Resort and Convention Center. The immensity of the place staggers the imagination. With close to three thousand rooms it's one of the largest hotels in the world. There's an enormous open-roofed central court, the Cascades Atrium, complete with trees, waterfalls, restaurants, and bars—and the vast atrium can easily disorient you. Cathy and I got lost five or six times during the weekend, and so did Kevin.

We settled into our separate rooms and took time off to relax. We had plans to meet Kevin a few hours later. I had told Cathy she could order room service, but when I called her twenty minutes before our scheduled meeting with my agent, she didn't answer her phone. I went down to the conference center alone.

Talk about taking over your life! The NACA marketplace hall looked like a circus. Picture a convention room larger than a football field, filled with innumerable rows of tables, like booths at an amusement park where you can throw darts and try to win prizes. These booths were staffed by college lecture agents, and they were set up with poster advertisements of the comedians, musicians, lecturers, and performers that they represented. The hall was filled with hundreds of people when I first entered, and later when the students arrived it would hold over a thousand. I made my way through the crowd, looking for Kevin's booth. I was gawking at all the other display tables I passed: some had videos running, and others were designed to attract students by letting them perform some fun activity, such as getting their photo taken, making a plaster cast of their face, or having their handwriting analyzed. Many booths had stacks of giveaways to entice students. There were free CDs, books, condoms, candy, and even stuffed animals, including little toy bears, dogs, and dolls. The booths measured fifteen to twenty feet in length and the agents decorated them with black, red, or white tablecloths. Suddenly out of the din of the hundreds of voices, I heard someone calling my name.

"Billy!. . . Billy, over here!"

Down at the end of a long row of tables, Kevin was standing in front of our booth, waving to me.

"Where's your friend?"

"I don't know," I said. "She didn't answer her phone."

Kevin explained the way he organized the booth for the Contemporary Issues Agency. On the wall behind our tables he attached posters for his most popular acts. The agency specialized in lectures about subjects like the legalization of marijuana, how to avoid abusing alcohol, subliminal advertising, and diversity—all topics that colleges were currently buying. I spent the next twenty minutes hooking up our posters and arranging publicity material on the tables. Then we cut lengths of string and hung the larger banners on the back wall. Our booth was set up in a U-shape, with the opening of the U facing the aisle so that people would be encouraged to enter and talk with Kevin to find out more about the acts he represented.

"Your showcase is scheduled tomorrow afternoon at one p.m., right after lunch break, so when the students come in tonight it might be a good idea to approach some of them and ask if they'd like to be in the demonstration."

"Are they going to come into this hall?"

"Yes, lots of them."

"And they're going to walk by the booth?"

"Of course."

"Okay, I'll be right back. I have an idea."

Kevin was surprised when I returned a minute later with a little stuffed dog. I cut four feet of string and made a noose and tied it around the dog's neck. Kevin gave me a quizzical look.

"What's that for?"

"You'll see."

An announcement came over the public address system:

"The marketplace will open in two minutes."

Kevin glanced at his watch.

"They're going to open the doors. I want to say hello to a friend of mine. If anyone comes to the booth, tell them I'll be right back to answer any questions." He handed me a booklet listing all the schools. "Give them a publicity packet, but be sure to put a check mark next to their name in this listing. That way we can follow up with them later, okay?"

After Kevin left, I looked down the row toward the entrance. I was stunned by what I saw. Hundreds of kids were standing immediately outside the doors. Six or seven security guards were making sure they didn't enter, and these officers were checking identification and only admitting agents. Then the announcer came on the loudspeaker again:

"The marketplace is open!"

All of a sudden the doors swung wide and hundreds of college students poured into the space. Droves of them began walking by our booth, but they weren't looking at any of our posters. That's when I put my plan into action. I stepped to the edge of the booth, where people were passing by continuously, and I dangled my toy dog from the end of the string. It bounced up and down on the floor. Three girls were walking by and they slowed to look at it.

"My dog is dead," I said.

Their faces dropped in surprise.

"Dead?"

"Yes, it died," I said.

Then, realizing the ludicrousness of the statement, they started laughing.

"Did you hear about the *Art of Kissing* show?" I asked.

They looked up from the dog to me, their faces registering astonishment.

"It's a show where students from your campus demonstrate thirty different types of romantic kisses onstage. We're doing a showcase tomorrow. Do you want to be in the show?"

One of the girls was beaming with interest. She had responded exactly as I had hoped.

"Are you kidding?" she said.

"Look," I said, handing her a flyer. "This is your ticket to be in the show. You don't even need a partner. We'll provide boys for you—and we always let the *girls* pick the guys they like."

"Oh my god!"

"Laura, you're not going to do it, are you?" one of the girls said.

Laura grabbed her friend's arm and shook it, saying, "Luke is here. Maybe he'll do it with me."

"What's your name?" I said, even though I knew her name was Laura. I wanted her to give me her name and see me write it down. This way she'd feel an obligation to show up for the rehearsal. After doing so many shows, I knew it was always better to have more volunteers than you really needed because you could always turn people away if you had too many, but if you didn't have enough it was impossible to get them to volunteer at the last minute.

Kevin returned to the booth and started talking with

the girls. While he was doing that, I dangled my dog into the stream of passersby again, and before long I hooked two guys from Salt Lake Community College to be in the showcase. After an hour of working like this, I had more than thirty names on my list.

Kevin was on the phone with his wife: "Billy's getting them into the booth. You won't believe what he does. He has a stuffed dog on a string . . ."

I smiled to myself, thinking what kind of crazy images must be going through Jayne's mind.

Fifteen minutes later the announcer spoke again over the public address system.

"The marketplace is closed!"

Droves of people began walking out of the hall. Some of them waved goodbye and said they would see us tomorrow. So! I would have my couples after all.

"Kevin," I said as we were walking out together, "you didn't tell me that NACA is like a circus."

He smiled. And I knew what he was thinking: Yes, it's a circus all right, and *you're* the circus act.

Next morning Kevin called at ten o'clock and told me to meet him in the auditorium. We had to be on time for my sound check. After I got off the phone I called Cathy. She apologized for falling asleep the night before and said she was tired and would miss the showcase too. My blood pressure hit the roof, especially after I had paid for her flight and hotel room—but I held my tongue. I told her everything was okay and that we'd catch up with her in the booth at four o'clock. Then I headed out, with half an hour to spare, looking for the performance auditorium. I wanted to be sure I didn't miss my appointment, though I didn't understand why Kevin was so insistent that the sound check be done on time. At all the schools I went to the sound check was a half-hearted affair, with students showing up to help me with it in their own good time.

I was surprised when I entered the auditorium and saw that the place was immense, with a capacity of over a thousand. But what really surprised me was that unlike at colleges, where I might have one or two students helping me, this venue was staffed with twenty lighting and sound technicians as well as a stage director. I had a team of energetic and knowledgeable people in black T-shirts at my beck and call.

"Do you want a spotlight?"

"What do you need for music?"

"How do you want house lights set?"

"What do you need onstage: chairs, props, just name it."

Suddenly I started to get excited, and now I understood why Kevin had insisted I be on time. Yes, this was the circus, and I was the circus act—but at least now they had trained technicians running the show. Having these experts assist me was like being in a television studio where you're surrounded by professionals. Not surprisingly, sound check proceeded without a hitch: the two techs working the audio board understood my sound cue checklist perfectly—something that had never happened at any school. The only thing that unnerved me was the oversize digital countdown timer positioned at the foot of the stage. I knew I had only twenty minutes to do the show, and I could feel the pressure mounting.

My showcase was scheduled for one o'clock, and I belatedly realized that I had scheduled rehearsal at lunchtime. I started to worry that my demonstrators would decide to have lunch instead of rehearse. But a few minutes before noon Laura showed up, just as she had promised. Before long many other volunteers ambled into the backstage area and I had to turn some of them away: "I'm sorry, we only have room for five couples onstage."

I also had the luxury of rehearsing my demonstrators twice. When I did the show at schools I never had time to rehearse more than once. But with a twenty-minute showcase you can squeeze in two rehearsals, which was wonderfully reassuring for me as a director.

By this time the auditorium was packed to overflowing and other artists had already started doing their show-cases. Quietly, I led my demonstrators into the theater and we sat in the audience, about fifteen rows from the front, waiting for our cue. More than a thousand people filled the auditorium, many standing in the back. A girl onstage talked about how she had been raped on a date, and then she explained how to deal with date rape. She received polite applause. There was one more act before us, a comedian, and I was glad that he would be light-ening the mood. I whispered to my demonstrators, reminding them to get ready, and ten minutes later I gave them a signal and we slipped out of our seats and rendez-voused behind the curtain. The stage manager held his finger to his lips, cautioning us not to disturb the current performer. Finally the comedian told his last joke and the audience applauded. It was our turn! Without delay, my demonstrators stepped in front of the curtain and sat onstage in their chairs. The master of ceremonies was already introducing me. Everything was rushing ahead like clockwork.

The spotlight came on, just as I had instructed the

light man to do it, hitting me in the face and, incidentally, blinding me. I ran through my introduction. When I moved out of the direct glare of the spot I could see students sitting in the front row. There were a lot of kids on the floor, too, jammed up close to the stage to get a better view. I recognized one of them.

"You didn't volunteer yesterday," I ad-libbed. "You're missing a good kissing opportunity."

The audience giggled. The house was alive and responding to all my material in a positive way. But when I glanced at the clock my heart froze. No time to lose! That red digital monster was counting down the seconds. It said 15:37.

I had already eaten up five minutes! I had to move faster. I turned to my demonstrators and got them up on their feet, in profile for the initial lip contact. The audience was mesmerized, leaning forward in their seats. They had never seen anything like it. When my couples did that first kiss, well—the crowd went wild, just as they had on college campuses.

Now I started to realize why Kevin had flown to Boston to rehearse me. Timing a showcase is critical. With only twenty minutes you have to do everything without delay. For example, I had no time to walk out into the house and behind the audience like I always did during my full shows. There was no time for questions and answers. Everything was *bam! bam! bam!* But that made for one of the most exciting performances of my career. When it was over and the audience broke into thunderous applause I didn't realize what that really meant.

But when I got back to our booth in the marketplace it hit me, and it hit me hard: our booth was jam-packed with students who had seen the showcase and loved it. It was so unique, so sexy, they wanted to book the show right then and there. Kevin was swamped with kids and directors of student activities. Ninety minutes later he turned to me as the marketplace was closing, and he smiled.

"Do you realize that you booked twelve shows, and we have strong interest from ten others? You just earned $30,000."

"Thirty thousand!"

"We raised your fee."

"And I didn't even have to use the dog to get them into the booth this time."

Kevin laughed . . . and I laughed all the way back to my hotel room. Then at eight o'clock we had yet another marketplace—the last of the day—and Cathy finally showed up. She had taken a nap and looked ravishing.

"What do you want me to do?" she said.

"I don't know. Ask Kevin."

"Kevin, what should I do?"

Kevin turned to her.

"Nothing special. Just tell people about the show if they have any questions."

When the marketplace opened our booth quickly became swamped with interested schools again. Whenever one of the colleges expressed strong interest or booked the show, Kevin taped a yellow ticket to the front of our booth. As the evening progressed, we had so many yellow tickets that it looked festive.

The dynamics in the booth were a little different this time. The boys all wanted to talk with Cathy.

At one point she took me aside and said, "They think if they book the show they're going to be kissing *me*."

"Tell them you'll come on the road with me and they'll see you again at the show."

She laughed.

"But don't make false promises," I said.

Kevin was in a great mood as he continued filling out strong interest forms. We left the conference smiling at the way things had worked out for us. Even Cathy was happy since I had promised that she could be my driver at the new bookings in Massachusetts, Connecticut, and New Hampshire. She would be earning extra cash and all she had to do was chauffeur me to local gigs. But when we returned to Boston College things quickly took an unexpected turn for the worse, and that smile got wiped right off my face.

CHAPTER SIXTEEN

THE SPANKING KISS

I CONTINUED RIDING THAT WAVE OF EUPHORIA in 1998 after we got back from Nashville. Cathy had enrolled in my fall vocabulary-building class, Techniques of Precise Expression. Not only was I a highly sought-after speaker on the college lecture circuit, I was also a popular teacher at Boston College. Other professors knew about my work and would ask to sit in and observe from time to time so that they could see how I worked my legendary magic in the classroom.

The secret to my success can be summed up quite succinctly: it was a simple matter of having fun myself. I told my students that if I didn't enjoy it, I wouldn't teach. I also told them, "I love teaching so much that I would do it even if they didn't pay me."

"We don't believe you!" one boy yelled.

But it was the truth, and I assured them that I loved what I was doing. The vocabulary class was so popular that it regularly drew close to a hundred students each semester. This always gave me a good pool of actors to cast in my skits. But I was heading for a fall and I didn't see it coming until it was too late. The problem was that

I had become overconfident; all the applause on the road with the kissing show had made me forget that I was teaching at a Jesuit university.

"This is the Canadian *Today* show calling."

I was on the phone with another television producer, this one from *Canada AM*, the most highly viewed morning show in the country.

"We would love to get some footage of your kissing show, which we've heard so many good things about."

"But I don't have anything scheduled right at the moment."

"Isn't there some way that we could bring our camera crew to film you directing some kids?"

Of course! I had more than a hundred students in my vocabulary class. Every week I would have two of my own video cameras rolling during the class because I recorded our vocabulary skits, and I also was so egotistical that I liked seeing myself teaching, so I usually told the camera operators to focus on me. What trouble could I get into if a few more cameras showed up? I didn't even ask permission from the dean.

"I teach a vocabulary class, and you're invited to come and film inside the classroom."

"Could you get some students to demonstrate?"

"I'm sure they'd love to."

That Thursday I prepared my students for the television cameras. They looked excited. This was certainly something different, and it would give them a break from having to listen to me pontificate about vocabulary. Several of them also volunteered to do the on-camera demonstrations, which was exactly what I needed. The class ran from six thirty to eight forty-five p.m. At seven o'clock a young woman and three men arrived from the Canadian television show. The woman was the segment producer, and the guys were camera operators and sound men.

"If any of you want to leave during our filming, that's okay," I told my class. But none of them left their seats. I smiled to myself. They all wanted to see what was going to happen.

I instructed my volunteers—just as if we were rehearsing for a kissing show—to stand in the front of the room. The producer said they would like to film three different kisses, so I suggested the neck kiss, lip-o-suction, and the biting kiss, during which guys give their partners a little love nip on the earlobe. I thought that filming would only take half an hour, but as with all television productions, they lied about that. They wound up staying more than ninety minutes, and there were cables, wires, and lights everywhere. So that ended all work for the night and I had to tell the class that we would pick up where we left off with our vocabulary words next week.

But when I walked into the office a week later, Cheryl gave me a dark look.

"Father would like to see you."

"Really?"

I never suspected that I would get in trouble again, but as soon as I entered the dean's office I could see that it was serious.

"This is the second time," he began. "First it was that debacle in your summer class. Now you had a Canadian television show in the room and you directed your students in additional kissing demonstrations. Two girls from the class complained. Honestly, this kind of behavior simply can't continue. You're risking your job."

Dean Woods was a great guy, and he was in my corner all the way, I knew. So I felt bad about putting this damper on his enthusiasm for my class. I apologized profusely and assured him that it would never happen again.

But week by week I had to devise new skits that would entertain my students and that would also be interesting for me. It so happens that at the time I had been reading a biography about Sigmund Freud, and I had come across the intriguing fact that his daughter Anna fantasized about being spanked. In a flash I envisioned a new story-line, which would entail doing a series of scenarios about the father of psychoanalysis. The Freud theme would also be used for our final skits at the end of the semester, which we would videotape. Throughout the rest of the fall I wrote a series of skits centered around Sigmund Freud and his followers, including Wilhelm Reich, Sandor Ferenczi, Carl Jung, and Freud's youngest daughter, Anna. But the initial skit I dreamed up was the most outrageous; in fact, it was so scandalous I almost hesitated to do it, and I worried whether I could even get any girl to volunteer to portray Anna Freud.

The scene would be set in Freud's living room, where he would set up a huge opaque screen. At the rear of the screen he would place a spotlight so that anyone who stepped behind the screen would project a silhouette onto it. Freud would stand in front of the screen and instruct his daughter Anna to sit before him and confess her inner-most thoughts. Meanwhile, two students would act out Anna's fantasies behind the screen so that their silhouettes could be seen by the entire class. Anna at first wouldn't want to participate in her father's latest test, but Freud would force her to reveal what was in her mind. Under pressure from him she would admit that she envisioned that she was kneeling down, that a man was standing behind her with a raised hand, and that she eventually received a thorough spanking.

It may be hard to understand why I decided to do this provocative skit, especially after being called on the carpet by the dean for bringing suggestive demonstrations into class. But I thought my students would love it. It seemed like something straight out of a Molière comedy: slapstick perhaps, but ultimately in good comedic tradition.

The big question was: Who could I get to be spanked? When I arrived early for class with the cameras, a few of the guys were already in the room. One of them, Tommy Atkinson, whose nickname was Bunker, asked if he could be my front desk assistant.

"Listen, Tommy, I have a crazy skit for today."

"Sure, tell me about it."

Tommy had one of the most upbeat personalities of any student I ever worked with. He was extremely friendly and also looked like a movie star.

"Okay, here it is. I need a girl to get spanked in one of the skits."

"Get Cathy for it, Professor. She'll do it."

"You think so?"

"Sure. I'll ask her."

"Thanks, Tommy. And could you be the one to spank her?"

"Of course! I'd love to."

As soon as Cathy waltzed into the room, Tommy approached her. A few seconds later she burst out laughing. Tommy returned to the front desk and smiled.

"She's in like Flynn."

Before class began I instructed two students to hold a white sheet across the front desk. Another boy would be operating the overhead projector behind the sheet, using it like a spotlight. I asked one of the girls to be Anna Freud: her name was Pearly Belmonte. She had an extremely cute and expressive voice, which I knew would be perfect for the role of Anna, especially when she had to scream. Blind to the obvious danger I was creating with this setup, I was secretly congratulating myself on being a casting genius.

I explained that the skit we would be doing that evening was based on the fact that Freud's daughter had spanking fantasies. We would be using the skit to practice one of our vocabulary words; I don't even remember the word we used in the skit now. In fact, I think I became so involved in directing this outrageous scenario that I didn't even use *any* of our words in it. Not surprisingly, this particular skit fascinated the class. The lights were shut off, Cathy and Tommy stepped behind the white sheet, and the student playing Freud—one of the most accomplished actors I had encountered at the college— instructed Anna to sit.

"I don't want to," Anna said.

"Tell me your thoughts," Freud said.

Anna sat and said, "Do I have to do this?"

"I insist!" her father said.

"I don't have any thoughts."

"Of course you do. Now tell me what you see in your head."

"I don't know . . . I see *myself.*"

Cathy stepped into the beam of the spotlight, her silhouette magnified to gigantic proportions.

"What are you doing?" Freud said.

"I'm squatting down," Anna said.

Cathy put her hands on the desk and knelt down, the silhouette of her backside clearly visible.

Members of the class started tittering.

"What else do you see?"

"There's a man behind me."

Tommy stepped into the spotlight, and his silhouette appeared behind Cathy's.

"What's the man doing?"

"His hand is raised—!"

Tommy raised his hand, and the silhouette of that raised hand elicited more laughter from the class.

"And he's—he's—he's *spanking* me!"

Tommy's hand flew down and whacked Cathy's backside. *Spank!* The class roared. But that wasn't the end of it.

"He's spanking me . . ." Anna repeated.

Tommy brought his hand down again and again, hitting Cathy so hard we could hear it echoing throughout the auditorium—*spank! spank! spank!*—while Cathy kept yelling, "Ow! ow! ow!" with each hit, and at the same time Anna kept speaking in an excited voice.

"And I *like* it!" Anna cried. "I like it!"

"Ow!" Cathy said behind the sheet. "Ow! . . . I'm not a bad girl! . . . Ow! . . . I'm not a bad girl!"

"I like it!" Anna repeated.

"Stop this!" Freud screamed. "Stop this immediately!"

Convulsing with laughter, the class burst into spontaneous applause. Never had they seen such an outrageous skit. I congratulated the actors and especially thanked Cathy for being such a good sport. We didn't get much work done during the rest of that class.

I guess it won't come as any surprise to you that the

next day I was reprimanded by Father Woods. I should have seen it coming. After all, he had warned me twice before, and I had promised to keep things calm and sedate in the class, but here I had gone and created a situation that was so scandalous and vulgar it almost demanded a reprimand.

"Two more students complained, Bill."

I was in the hot seat in his office again. His face was dead serious.

"You can't have students getting spanked in class."

He let those words sink in.

"But it was just for fun," I said. "And it was based on the fact that Freud's daughter liked to be spanked."

"I don't care," the dean said. "A couple of the girls in the class said they were traumatized by watching that scene. You have to promise not to do anything like this anymore or you're really risking your job. I like you, and you're an effective teacher, but you must calm down."

"Very well," I said. "I'll remove that skit from the final performance of the Freud movie we're going to make."

But when I returned home that night, don't you know that I was inspired by what had happened in class? My scenario had provoked such an outpouring of laughter and applause from my students that I knew I'd struck upon an entertaining idea. You can't please everyone, I was telling myself, and you shouldn't stifle your imaginative energies by trying to, either. I was delighted with the reaction of the class to the spanking skit. Of course I was sorry that it had troubled my friend and longtime supporter, Dean Woods. I told myself in no uncertain terms that I would do right by him and calm the class down in the future, but I certainly wasn't going to let the opportunity slip by to use that spanking concept in my kissing show. The audience at Boston College was representative of college students across the country, and if my class found spanking funny, audiences at other colleges could be expected to respond in a similar way. I didn't worry about the fact that it might shock or annoy one or two people.

The next time I went on the road I explained to the young woman who was the director of student activities that we had a new skit, and that I was excited to try it for the first time on her campus. I described it briefly to her, and she smiled and said it sounded fine. Lucky for me I was doing the show in Massachusetts, where some of my most liberal audiences happened to be located. During rehearsal I downplayed the sensational aspects of the skit for the demonstrators because I didn't want to alarm them.

"We're going to do a spanking kiss, where the boys spank the girls during a romantic kiss—just a playful little love pat." They seemed to be taking this announcement tolerably well, but when you look at someone's face you can't always figure out what they're really thinking, and I wanted to reassure them, so I added, "If you can't do it, that's okay, just let me know." By giving them an opportunity to decline participation, I calmed their nerves. All of the volunteers decided to go ahead with the skit, which was precisely what I had hoped they would do.

That night I introduced the spanking kiss to the first college audience like this:

"Ladies and gentlemen, we're now going to show you a fun way to kiss your partner and also add a little aggressive love play into your make-out sessions. Demonstrators, please stand facing your partners." My volunteers faced each other. "The boy steps up to the girl and gets so close that his pelvis is pressed against hers, and then he puts one arm around her waist and kisses her. At the same time he raises his other hand behind her back—high, high, up to the heavens." The boys raised their hands high. Seeing this, the audience began to anticipate what was going to happen next, and just as they had in my vocabulary class, they began to giggle. I finished my narration, with these words: "Then he brings his hand down *fast and hard* for a loud spank!"

Roars of laughter.

The spanking kiss became an instant sensation at the first campus, and it continued to be one of the high points of the show at other schools. Colleges in the Northeast and on the West Coast responded well to the new spanking kiss, but when I traveled to conservative southern schools I was often required to keep this risqué scenario out of the performance. I felt bad for those audiences at southern schools who would never see this skit, and as a result I often resorted to at least describing it for them. But describing a spanking kiss can't do it justice . . . you've simply got to see it to believe it.

CHAPTER SEVENTEEN

STAND-UP AND THE KISSING SHOW

"PROFESSOR, I DON'T MIND MAKING A FOOL of myself in your class." Cathy was walking through the Boston College parking lot with me one afternoon when she confessed this interesting fact about herself. "I don't know why," she continued. "But I'll do whatever I can to help you have a good lesson."

Later in the semester she proved to be an extremely capable actress, especially when I needed someone to do something out of the ordinary. It was in this way that she eventually became the most influential muse for the kissing show. I learned to test my ideas on her, and if they worked with the Boston College crowd they were likely to work for a national audience. Just to give you a couple of other examples, she performed improvised ballet in class, and she also wore a hooded robe to portray Death in a Halloween skit.

I used her ballet moves to choreograph a number of additions to the kissing show. In one skit, a boy and girl would see each other across a crowded dance floor and make eye contact for a sensual eye kiss, during which the lovers simply gazed at one another and flirted with their eyes. I also used ballet footwork to help girls glide across the stage toward their partners. I incorporated the Death character for a Halloween show, in which a boy had a nightmare and ended up kissing a female Death spirit. All these scenarios worked in the kissing show, and I had Cathy to thank for giving them their initial tryouts in class.

But having a college student as your muse can sometimes lead you into making a fool of yourself—that was always the danger. And I had the kind of reckless energy that compelled me to take those kinds of risks, always pushing my luck in an attempt to improve audience reaction. So when I got my next brainstorm I rushed it into production without considering any negative consequences it might cause. First thing I did was call my friend Bryant Alvarez to tell him what I was going to do. Bryant is an attorney whom I met while working at a real estate office in Newton, Massachusetts, when I was in law school.

"Don't do it, Bill!" he said.

"Why not? I think I'd enjoy trying stand-up."

"But what if you bomb?"

"I'm not afraid of that."

"But for the rest of your career you'll have an inferiority complex. You might not be able to speak in public anymore."

"I already have an inferiority complex," I said, "and I do fine speaking to audiences."

"Not funny."

"Trust me, I'm working on some good jokes."

Bryant thought for a minute, and then he offered his final argument: "I speak to groups all the time. They're elderly people who want estate planning advice. My method is simple: I just keep talking until I say something funny. I don't even plan it in advance; an idea just pops into my head while I'm talking, and I say it and people laugh. But I would *never* try stand-up. It's too risky."

When I got off the phone I told myself to ignore his advice. Bryant was smart, but he wasn't me. I knew what I could do and what I couldn't do. I bought a portable tape recorder, and whenever something funny occurred to me I would ad-lib into it. Then I transcribed these monologues and worked on making them shorter and punchier. At this time, in 1998, I also started visiting comedy clubs in Boston, Brookline, and Cambridge. While doing this I met Chance Langton, one of the most hilarious professional comedians I had ever seen. Chance used a lot of one-liners, and he had one specific joke that I loved above all his others. After he did his set, he would pause briefly, smile at the audience, and then say: "Are there any requests for any of the jokes I already told?" He usually killed them at the Comedy Studio, which was located over a Chinese restaurant in Harvard Square. Chance and I became friends, and he also became my mentor. I even took a class with him on comedy technique. Naturally, I also ran my jokes by Cathy.

In the summer of 1999 I had mailed a video on spec to an MTV producer, and although he didn't use it he suggested that I submit a few interstitials—short promos for the network—to their sister channel MTV2. I invited Cathy to act in one of these film projects, and during a break in shooting I tried one of my jokes on her. We were in the kitchen of the house that I had rented for the shoot, and I told her a silly story about how I used to get disciplined as a kid, put in the corner, spanked, and sent to bed early.

Cathy cracked up.

"You think it's funny?" I asked.

"Yes."

"How come?"

"'Cause I know exactly what that's like."

"Are you serious?"

"My father was a strict disciplinarian."

I think Cathy's strict upbringing and closeness with her dad had a major impact on her personality. Although she possessed a rebellious streak, she also had a pronounced tendency to act extremely compliant around men who had authority. For example, when I directed her in the MTV shoot or in class she slipped into an almost automaton-like state. She once told me, "I'd like to find a man who could tell me what to do, and I'd do it. But I'm afraid of that side of myself." In some ways she had a Jekyll and Hyde personality: when she wasn't being rebellious and bossy, she treated me like a father figure and respected my ideas and instructions. I respected her opinions too, so after she gave me this positive feedback on my joke I decided to lead off with it in the stand-up routine that I was developing. I planned to do my first performance in downtown Boston at an open mic night hosted by a local comedian. I set up my camcorder in the back of the room to record my show, and I sat waiting my turn. I had decided to use a new stage name for the set: Jack Hackensack. Folks, I was stunned because when I was announced people started laughing even before I walked up to the microphone. It turns out that they thought my name was funny, and let me tell you, it's a wonderful thing for a performer when an audience has a positive feeling about you before you even open your mouth. I was nervous, but I had spoken before so many audiences that I thought I might have an aptitude for doing live comedy. Unfortunately, I learned that my ability as a lecturer on the subject of kissing didn't exactly translate to the comedy arena.

That first stand-up experience got me a decent amount of laughs, but I felt naked on the stage. The problem was that I didn't have my kissing demonstrators up there with me. I even included a few jokes about kissing, but again I felt they would have worked better with the couples present. All the focus was on me at the comedy club, and even though I had rehearsed my material thoroughly and didn't forget any of my jokes, I didn't feel comfortable with the setup. In fact, when I compared myself with other young comedians who tried out their material at these open mics, I could see that they looked relaxed whereas I felt too nervous to enjoy it. Still, I pushed myself to perform seven or eight times in Boston, Cambridge, and New York. Ironically, about twenty years later Cathy started doing stand-up too—and she got more laughs than I did.

Now here's where stand-up harmed my speaking career. While researching material to add to my performance, I studied the work of successful comedians, including Woody Allen, Lenny Bruce, and Andrew Dice Clay. Clay had a technique of dealing with hecklers that I thought I could incorporate into my kissing show in the event that I encountered troublesome audience members. Most college crowds were friendly and polite, and up to that point I hadn't encountered any hecklers, but I wanted to be prepared just in case. His technique, which is used by many professional comedians, is to call the heckler an asshole. There are actually two common put-downs that the pros use: one is to insinuate that the heckler is a drunk or so intoxicated that he doesn't know what he's doing, and the other is to call him an asshole in hopes that he'll shut up.

Shortly after I started dabbling in the world of stand-up, I was booked to do a gig at a school that had a reputation for late-night parties, especially on weekends. My show was scheduled for Friday night, and when I started speaking, I immediately realized that this was a terrible crowd. Although the room was overflowing with about four hundred students, I couldn't hear myself talking because they were so noisy and disruptive. I figured I had to shut them down, and fast. The room had a balcony, and it too was filled to capacity with students. One girl yelled out some nonsense, and I looked up at her and used Clay's line.

"I think you're an asshole."

The room instantly became quiet.

"And by the end of the evening everyone here is going to think you're an asshole."

This shut the girl up, and she promptly left. So, in that sense, wouldn't you say I did the right thing?

Oh, *noooooooo*! Not by a long shot.

When I got home I received an angry call from Kevin.

"You're in trouble," he said. "The school wants its money back. You called one of the students an asshole."

"I know, but they were a bunch of drunks. I mean, you literally could not hear me talking even though I had a microphone. And I was worried for my demonstrators, the kids who had rehearsed for an hour. They weren't being treated right either."

"But you can't use that kind of language."

"Why not? I got the idea from Andrew Dice Clay. He's very big and he uses it."

"But he's a professional comedian working in night-clubs. He's not beholden to a college that paid him to speak to students."

We eventually had to settle with the school and give half their money back. That was the first mistake stand-up introduced into my show. The second mistake resulted from my curiosity about the history of comedy. I studied the ancient Greeks and Romans, and the tradition of the *commedia dell'arte*. I had started reading about the commedia, an Italian comedy technique, while I was an undergrad at Boston College. I had stumbled across books about it in the college library while I was researching mate-rial for a debate. I poured over these books on commedia characters and techniques and incorporated them into *Jane's First Love*, a Boston College Radio Theater soap opera that I directed from 1981 to 1997. It's important to understand that commedia involves specific routines, called *lazzi*, which the performers ad-libbed during their plays. The closest modern equivalent might be the routines of the Three Stooges, Abbott and Costello, and Laurel and Hardy. It just so happened that I had read about a lazzi that involved a man giving an enema to his horse. In this lazzi, two actors under a blanket play the role of the horse. I started to wonder whether I could incorporate something like that in the kissing show.

The only problem was that horses have nothing to do with kissing. But for the life of me, I wanted to use this lazzi. I was convinced it was so unique and so startling that if I could only figure out some way to incorporate it into my stage show, it would wow a college audience.

Eventually I figured out how to do it. I decided to stop the show midstream and tell an elaborate enema joke as if I were doing stand-up. Naturally, as I did with all my stand-up bits, I wrote it out, edited it, and rehearsed it at home to get the timing down. Then I took it out on the road for a test.

I tried it for the first time at an affluent school in the Midwest. I had already been there twice and always had a receptive audience—no one ever heckled me at this college. I always worked in the same venue too, a multi-purpose hall that seated five hundred. The performance area was a platform raised three feet off the floor. Right in the middle of the show I stopped the demonstrations and launched into my new routine.

"My first kiss was a disaster," I began. "I was going out with a nurse, and she told me to meet her in the hospital where she worked. The room I was waiting in had a barn door, one of those doors where you can open the top half. As I was waiting for her I overheard one of the teaching nurses instruct one of the students: 'You have three minutes to complete this test and give the man in the next room an enema.' Then a short wizened little guy entered the room carrying a rubber bag attached to a hose with a long nozzle. He approached me while I was leaning out the barn door waiting for Daisy, and he started fiddling with the back of my jacket. 'Get away from me,' I said. He replied in an almost incoherent voice: 'I'm supposed to take the test—' I pushed him away, but just then Daisy appeared on the other side of the door. I was trying to work up my courage to kiss her, when I heard the instructor telling the man: 'You're going to fail this test, *you have only two minutes left.*' While I was leaning forward to try and kiss Daisy, I felt this guy lifting my jacket again. I pushed him again, saying: 'Get the hell away from me.' Now Daisy was close enough to be kissed—I could smell her perfume—and my temperature started to go up. The nurse said: 'You have only *thirty seconds*.' I leaned over the barn door and put my tongue into Daisy's mouth—and at the same time the little creep lifted my jacket and put something into *me*. . . . And that's how I had my first kiss."

I received polite applause, but in my delusional ignorance I imagined that I was another Johnny Carson. Little did I realize that I had made a major gaffe. When I got home I heard it from Kevin.

"Bill, listen"—whenever he called me Bill instead of Billy it signaled trouble—"what the heck are you doing now—talking about an enema in a kissing show! You can't do that."

"But Kevin—"

"No excuses! It's just not acceptable."

"But it's a classic gag."

"I don't care."

"They use it all the time in the commedia."

"I don't care."

"They *laughed*."

"I don't care. Take it out of the show. These are college kids. Keep this show clean. It's our biggest act and I spent a lot of time with you making it right. Don't screw it up now."

CHAPTER EIGHTEEN

CORNELL

WHY IS IT THAT WHEN EVERYTHING SEEMS to be going right, things have a nasty habit of taking a turn for the worse? That's exactly what happened after I got chewed out by Kevin for my clowning in the Midwest. I decided to remove the risqué jokes from my show and be nice to everybody on the road, especially my audiences. When I got the offer from Cornell, Kevin reminded me not to screw things up since this school was buying two shows back to back on successive nights. I told myself to make sure that things went well at both events, but fate stepped in and completely ruined my plans.

Cornell scheduled the shows to be presented in two different locations: the first for graduate students on March 3, 2000, the second for undergrads the next night. I had performed for graduate students before, including a presentation for a medical college, and I was nervous because grad students are older, wiser, and usually less juiced up than college audiences. The kissing show could still work for an older crowd, but you had to be sensitive to the way grad students were taking it, and you had to be flexible enough to adapt your presentation on the fly.

So I expected the first performance to be challenging, and that's exactly how it played out.

The good thing about the first show was that one of the girls had terrific acting ability. She was also dressed in goth style, complete with black choker, thigh-high boots, and blue hair. Appearances aside, whenever you have a talented demonstrator it generates intense interest from your audience. As a director of stage plays I always had the opportunity to rehearse for weeks and bring out the best in my cast, but with the college show there wasn't any time to change their behavior before a performance, even if I wanted to make suggestions. So I had to rely on a certain amount of luck to find talented volunteers.

My graduate volunteers had a lot of energy and followed all my directions in the rehearsal, so I felt confident about the way the show would progress. The venue was a small black-box theater with a square platform raised six inches off the floor serving as the stage. Seventy-five folding chairs had been preset. About forty-five graduate students showed up, including a few people who looked like faculty. As expected, the audience was laid-back and had a more intellectual, wait-and-see attitude. They occasionally laughed and appeared to be entertained, but they didn't scream or jump out of their seats with excitement like most of my undergrad audiences. Fortunately, the talented demonstrator did a good job holding the attention of the crowd even during slower parts of the show, such as during the sliding kiss and the teasing kiss, where her playfulness captured everyone's attention.

For the sliding kiss, the guys knelt on their chairs and leaned over their partners to plant tiny little kisses on their bare arms and shoulders. If the girls weren't already wearing sleeveless outfits or short sleeves, I instructed them to roll up their sleeves and expose their arms so that the boys could do sliding kisses all the way up to their neck. During this skit the goth girl's over-the-top responses presented a special advantage because her partner was able to do the sliding kiss on her shoulder, which turned out to be one of the high points of the demonstration—she jumped unexpectedly out of her chair and landed on the floor.

During the teasing kiss the boys were supposed to stand at attention like the Queen's Guard and maintain a stoic, nonresponsive posture for one full minute while the girls kissed them any way they wished. Most guys can't remain motionless under such conditions, and the skit usually concluded with the boys breaking their military poses and succumbing to the girls.

In this instance the girl with acting talent had a powerful advantage over her boyfriend; all she had to do was stand in front of him for a few seconds until that striking image began to melt his nerves, then she stepped closer and all eyes in the audience zeroed in on her. Finally she placed one arm on his shoulder and the guy doubled up with laughter.

The next skit involved a group kiss, where the joke was that the demonstrators experienced a power outage at a party. I actually kept the lights on during this skit because I wanted the audience to see everything that happened. The students dropped to their knees and crawled around, as if in the dark, trying to find their partners. Then they ran into the wrong people and kissed *them*. Next the volunteers crawled into the audience! "You're in the show, too!" I cried into the microphone. "Here they come—

they can't see anything, and they're kissing *you*." With undergrad crowds this skit usually provoked excitement and laughter. They thought they might be kissed, and they saw their friends and roommates being kissed by the demonstrators.

All told, I would rate the graduate show at Cornel a B-plus on the excitement scale. After the performance I was a little disappointed. I started packing up my props, mulling over what I could have done better. That's when the director of student activities took me aside and told me something that really surprised me.

"A few years ago there was an orgy in Risley Hall, and of course everyone on campus knows about it. So during tomorrow night's show if you happen to mention Risley Hall during the group kiss, it might be funny."

I filed that little tidbit away in my mind. For the next show I was booked into a rectangular multipurpose room. The stage wasn't at the end of the hall, instead it was against the long wall. This meant that I would be closer to everyone; and to make things even more intimate I rearranged the chairs to form a tight curve at the ends so that people would be facing the stage instead of looking at a blank wall. The room was well lit and I knew that everyone would have a good view.

Since I always conducted a closed rehearsal, meaning no one not associated with the show was permitted to view it, I never saw the crowd until the last minute when we made our way to the stage. The moment we entered the venue after rehearsal was one of the best indicators of how the show would go. It was also an exciting time for me and the volunteers. If the room was filled to capacity and people were talking with one another, it was a good sign.

With this audience the excitement in the air was palpable. Every seat was occupied and kids were walking around in the back looking for a place to sit. More people kept pouring into the room, and additional folding chairs were being hurriedly carried in by the staff. Once my demonstrators took the stage the excitement level increased to an almost unbearable intensity. I loved talking to the audience before I was even introduced, which is a technique I learned from doing comedy shows. My friends who were professional comedians often chatted with people as they entered the venue, and in this way they got a sense of the crowd.

"All the seats are good," I joked. "Except the ones behind those columns with an obstructed view."

The organizer of the event asked if I would mind waiting a couple of minutes because they wanted to bring in additional chairs. This wasn't a problem for me: the more the better, in my opinion. Most people don't realize it, but almost all performers will tell you that larger crowds are easier to entertain than smaller ones. I used the extra minutes to talk with my volunteers, going from couple to couple and reassuring them that they were going to do a fabulous job.

Once the presentation got underway I could sense immediately that this was going to be an entirely different ball game from the graduate show the previous night: laughter ran through the sea of faces with every joke, and the positive vibe in the room was contagious. I drew energy from the crowd and gave it everything I had. When I came to the group kiss I waited until the demonstrators were crawling around, groping for each other, and then I said:

"Just like Risley Hall."

The room exploded! I didn't have to say the word *orgy*. Every person in attendance knew the reference. The rest of the show flowed perfectly, right up to the concluding scenario, that high-octane car kiss. I still have a video of the show, and I'm caught on camera raising my hand high to remind the boys how to spank the girls. We closed to thunderous applause and a standing ovation, something I had never achieved before.

I was drenched with sweat but elated as I thanked my volunteers, shook their hands, and then began to collect my props. While I was doing this, the organizer of the event approached. I thought he was going to congratulate me, but he looked serious.

"Some members of the lesbian club asked if they could talk with you."

I never saw the trouble coming; instead, I thought they probably loved the show so much they wanted to book me for their club too.

"Okay," I said.

I stepped off the stage and four girls walked over. They already had their coats on and looked glum.

"We understand that you got a lot of laughs," one of them said. "But you didn't have any gay students in the show."

"No gay students volunteered," I said.

The guy who booked the show nodded.

I had an open-door policy and I would have included a same-sex couple if they had volunteered.

"But you should have them," one of the other girls piped up.

"That's right," the third girl said.

The first girl concluded with a remark that shocked

me: "The show was homophobic, and I don't think we should have spent student funds on it."

I couldn't believe my ears. At many schools same-sex couples *had* volunteered and had been included. Maybe their objections were based on a misunderstanding of the fact that I *did* have an open-door policy and that they could have been in the show if they had volunteered. But even when the director of student activities and I explained this policy to them twice, they still looked like they wanted to keep arguing with us.

After thoroughly entertaining this audience and sending more than five hundred students away happy, I naturally expected that I'd be invited back to Cornell the next year or the year after. Many schools regularly brought me back year after year to do the kissing show, and at those colleges I would sometimes meet the same kids in the audience—they had enjoyed it so much the first time that they returned to see it again. But I was never invited back to Cornell.

One day I asked Kevin about it.

"How come they never bring me back?" I said.

"They never will, Billy."

"But why? I killed them."

"Because of those protesters."

CHAPTER NINETEEN

EAST COAST COLLEGES

EVERY TIME I THINK ABOUT THE CRAZINESS
that occurred on March 17, 1999, when I went up to Endicott College in Beverly, Massachusetts, I find it hard to
believe that it really happened to me. The problem is that
I'm a terrible driver and always have been. During my first
driving lesson, which I received from my mother, I backed
into a tree. A few years later I was trying to impress a girl
by driving her home and I crashed into the car in front of
us. I had to borrow money from my date to pay for the
accident. And then, of course, there was the incident with
Cathy and the toll booth.

My problem with driving stems from my limited
eyesight. When I was in my early thirties my ophthalmol-
ogist informed me I didn't have normal three-dimensional
vision. "What's the matter with you?" he said. "Why
can't you see in three dimensions? How long have you
had this issue?"

Listen, I'm thinking, *you're the doctor, you're
supposed to be telling* me.

"Doctor," I said, "I just came in here to get my vision
checked. I have no idea."

"Do you see things the way I do?"

"That's not my question," I said. "All I care about is getting a new pair of glasses."

"But the way *you* see things and the way *I* see things could be totally different."

"Just fix me up with a prescription."

My doctor's office happened to be across the street from the Boston University philosophy department. He had professors coming in every day talking with him about deep issues. I saw one guy in the waiting room reading *Being and Time.*

"Do you realize," my doctor said, "that Sartre saw the world in a completely different way from you and me?"

"Doc, I didn't come in here to talk about Jean-Paul Sartre." I expressly used Sartre's full name to show him that I was on his level when it came to philosophy but that I wasn't in the least bit interested in talking about it with him. "I need glasses." I said. "I can't drive unless you make my eyes twenty-twenty, understand? I have to be able to see when I'm on the road, and I'm on the road a lot doing shows."

"The question is—" He paused and looked up as if contemplating the ineffable mysteries of life. When he continued he appeared to be baffled: "Can any of us see things the way anyone else sees them?"

"I'm not interested in philosophy," I said. "And if you don't give me a new pair of glasses, I'm *out* of here."

In actuality I *was* interested in philosophy, but I didn't want to waste time gabbing about it with my eye doctor. I got up and was about to leave the office when his secretary called me back. She was around twenty-five and was wearing a navy-blue silk blouse and a gray wool skirt that came down to her knees. This look struck me as eminently professional, and I calmed down and decided to listen to what she had to say. She apologized for the doctor's distracted behavior, and she held up a prescription that she wanted me to take.

"He's got a lot on his mind," she said.

"I appreciate that," I said. "But are you sure this is the right prescription? I have a very special case; he said I have difficulty seeing in three dimensions."

The young woman studied the script and then handed it to me. "Yes, that's the right prescription for you. This will let you drive and correct your eyesight to twenty-twenty."

"But what about the three dimensions?"

"I'm sure you'll be fine. You don't need to see in three dimensions to drive."

"Really?"

"We have patients with only one eye, and *they* can drive."

"So this'll work for me?"

"I'm sure it will."

I got my new glasses, but I was still nervous about driving. Remember, the doctor himself, the guy who was supposed to be the expert, had said the reason I was a poor driver was that I lacked normal binocular vision. He had even given me a special vision test, which consisted of several drawings you were supposed to look at to see if they appeared three-dimensional. To me, they had all looked perfectly flat, which is why, I presume, he had said I had very poor—"abnormally low," he phrased it—three-dimensional vision. But the secretary had said everything would be fine. So who should I believe, the doctor or the secretary? I had to admit that even though the doctor had annoyed me with all his talk about Sartre, I probably should give his opinion greater weight because, after all, it was he who had gone to medical school, right? But being the credulous chump that I am, and wanting to believe the word of this enchanting young woman, I decided that I would try the new glasses by driving. And here's where I made a crucial decision—I would only drive if I couldn't find a student driver. In other words, I would get behind the wheel myself, but only in the unlikely event that none of my students was available to drive me to my next gig.

It just so happened that when I announced the driving opportunity, none of my students was available on the night I had to go to Endicott College. Even Cathy couldn't do it. I offered her $355, but she had a test that night for her new career as a certified personal trainer. So what was I supposed to do? That's when I made the decision to try my new glasses by renting a car and driving to Beverly, Massachusetts, by myself.

Oh, brother, I should have known something was wrong as soon as I put on that new pair of eyeglasses! If you wear glasses you know how a new prescription can make everything look a little screwy at first, until you get used to them. Well, these babies did that all right, and then some. Not only did the world look too sharp and angular when I slipped them on, but they gave me a headache as I walked to the Avis car rental building on Commonwealth Avenue. I had half a mind to go into my eye doctor's office unannounced and tell him that his prescription constituted a serious form of malpractice, but I didn't want to make a fool of myself in front of his secretary. It occurred to me that if I managed to use these newfangled spectacles then maybe I could thank her and see if I could get a date with her. Brainless wonder that I am, I marched right into the car rental place and boldly asked for a vehicle.

"Give me a small car."

"A small car?"

"Yes, because I need to be able to park easily."

"All our cars park easily."

"But you don't understand." Through my new glasses, the girl behind the rental counter looked so edgy she might have been a cartoon. She certainly didn't look three-dimensional. "I need a small vehicle because, um . . ." I stuttered to a stop. I didn't want to admit that I was a terrible driver. I didn't want her to know I needed a small car to avoid accidents. "I need a small vehicle to save on gas."

"All our vehicles are gas efficient."

"Just please give me a smallish car, okay?"

She looked in her inventory.

"I can give you a Chevy Camaro."

I was unfamiliar with cars and didn't know what this one looked like or how large it was.

"It's the smallest *item* we currently have."

I liked the way she pronounced the word: *eye-dumb*. It was really cute and kind of hot, and I thought she might be flirting with me.

"Okay, I'll take it."

"Just have a cigarette and I'll get the tank filled up and we'll drive it up front for you."

"I don't smoke."

The truth is that I really *did* smoke, having relapsed after quitting, but I wanted her to think that I was health conscious. Five minutes later a sky-blue monster of a car rolled up outside the rental window, and the girl came around the counter and handed me the keys.

"Can you—er—just show me—"

"What is it?" she said.

"I mean, can you give me an overview?"

"Of the Camaro?"

"If you don't mind."

"Well, I'm not supposed to leave the desk to do that, but if all you want is a quick overview—"

"And do you have an extra aspirin?"

She showed me how to put the key into the ignition and turn the car on. That was all I thought I really needed. I mean, to drive you just have to switch the vehicle on and take to the road, right?

The main issue I had with the Camaro, though, was that the front of the car was a mile long. The thing had been designed, I later learned, to compete with the Mustang, so it had to look like a sports car. I started the vehicle and inched slowly forward to the edge of the rental lot and then jammed on the brakes, engaged the parking mechanism, and got out to examine the car. I needed to get accustomed to the dimensions of the thing, but with my new glasses every angle of the Camaro looked extra sharp, and the entire vehicle appeared so enormous that I wasn't even sure I could navigate it out their gate onto Commonwealth Avenue and into traffic. I glanced at my watch. It was already five thirty, and the show was scheduled to start at eight. I had to be there at six to do a sound check.

"What's the matter?"

The girl had come out of the office.

"Nothing," I said. "I'm just checking the car before taking it onto the road."

When I finally got rolling down Commonwealth Avenue, I started to sweat profusely. From where I was sitting I could not for the life of me tell where the car ended in the front, or, more importantly, on the passenger side. I was a nervous wreck—I never knew whether I'd be sideswiping parked cars or vehicles in the other lanes. To compensate for this problem, I hit upon what I considered an ingenious solution: I beeped my horn—a quick little toot—to alert other drivers to my presence. *Beep! Beep!* Just a friendly little "Hi, I'm here!" to keep them away from me. *Beep! Beep!* and then I'd drive for about a minute or two, and tap out another couple of beeps. In this fashion I managed to get onto Storrow Drive and begin the arduous trek up to the college.

Miracle of miracles, I made it all the way to Endicott College and parked the car. When I got out I was dizzy and drenched in nervous sweat. I stumbled into the venue, my vision still distorted. I went through the motions of the rehearsal like a zombie, and the show passed by like a disturbing dream. Still, I was proud of myself for completing the performance, and all I had to do now was drive home. When I got back on the road, I repeated the beeping procedure, crawling along at under forty miles per hour. Other motorists gave me ugly stares as they zoomed past. By the time I arrived back at Avis, the rental office had closed and their gate was locked, so I was forced to try and park on Commonwealth Avenue, an almost impossible challenge because I had no accurate sense of the Camaro's dimensions and I needed to keep getting out to check how close I was to the curb. And then at the last moment I accidentally stepped too hard on the accelerator as I was backing into the spot, and I crashed into the car behind me.

"Damn!"

I got out to inspect the damage. When I saw what I had done my heart sank: there was a dent the size of a fist in the Camaro's rear fender. The car behind me must have been made out of hardened steel because it looked unaffected. Just my luck, I thought—I drove all the way to Endicott and all the way back without incident, and then at the last second I screwed it up and crashed the rental car. I started pacing back and forth on the sidewalk trying to figure out what to do. It was getting dark, and the more I looked, the harder it became to see the dent. Maybe I had exaggerated it in my mind, I thought. And maybe the Avis girl wouldn't notice. I walked home and fell into a restless slumber.

But I got a rude awakening when the phone woke me up at eight the next morning.

"Yeah, um, hello?"

"You banged up the rental car," a girl's voice droned into my sleep-clogged brain. *Who the heck is this?* I was wondering. "That *item* is noted on your account now." Pronounced "eye-dumb." *That* answered my question—the Avis girl. "Plus you parked in a 'No Parking' zone, and the vehicle was towed. We have to charge you a repair and towing fee, which will come to $275.65, okay? These fees will appear on your next credit card statement."

I swallowed my pride and decided right then and there that I would never drive to a school by myself again. But out of adversity and chaos comes order, does it not? Out of mindless stupidity can emerge some of the best ideas.

At least it has often been my experience that when I crash and burn I can sometimes rise again like the phoenix, somehow inspired with a brand-new brainstorm. And so it happened in this instance. That unfortunate conclusion to my Endicott road trip led directly to one of my best kissing show ideas.

The fender-smashing incident in front of the Avis rental office made me think about the possibility of adding a car crash to the show. And of course the most appropriate spot for such an addition would be at the conclusion of the performance as an enhancement to the car skit finale. I reasoned that it would be funny if the girls climbed onto the boys' laps and kissed them so passionately that they caused the guys to almost have a car accident—not a real accident, mind you, just a near accident. But why not go all the way and let the boys crash their cars, the way I had done? The answer to this reasonable question had been hammered home to me when I was thirteen and sitting in my high school English class. I'll never forget Mr. Beasley, our strict but competent English teacher, covering the ancient Greek theory of tragedy.

"What do you think Aristotle said is more effective?" Mr. Beasley asked the class. "If the dramatist makes a character suffer a catastrophe, or if he makes the character narrowly miss suffering a catastrophe?"

I raised my hand, and he called on me.

"Missing the catastrophe is better," I said.

He'd been looking at his book where he had his finger in the margin, preparing to quote Aristotle and correct me. But he raised his eyes and his jaw went slack.

"Yes!" he said. "That's right."

He proceeded to explain for the class: "If a dramatic

character *almost* suffers a catastrophe, Aristotle said that the audience would put *themselves* into the hero's shoes and would feel the narrow miss much more intensely than if the catastrophe actually happened to someone else, and as a result a near catastrophe can make an audience experience a personal catharsis of intense feeling."

This was exactly the effect I was hoping to achieve by having the girls *almost* make the boys crash. Plus, to have a real crash would have been a downer, and the kissing show had to end on an upbeat note. Averting a crash at the last second would leave the audience exhilarated. The final visual impression they would take out of the theater with them would be an image of the girls kissing the boys in that car scene—after almost making them crash.

I first introduced the car crash—the *almost* crash, that is—at Temple University in Philadelphia. I had performed at Temple numerous times, and it was always a fun school to speak at because the students were liberal and I could do all my provocative skits, including the shower kiss, the vacuum kiss, the spanking kiss, and everything else, and they never complained about any of it. It just so happened that on the night I was to perform the car crash, two different television crews showed up at the venue to cover the show.

The performance was staged in a cozy little area next to the campus hamburger stand. Students hung out at the spot to talk and socialize, so everything appeared friendly and welcoming in the space, which helped create a relaxed atmosphere for the event. Egomaniac that I am, and always hungry for media attention, I had started sending faxes to local newspapers, radio stations, and television producers about my upcoming shows, inviting them to cover the event for their nightly news. I had learned this publicity tactic from Lauren Harper at the Boston Arts Group, and it paid rich dividends since I was quite successful in drumming up media interest and coverage for the kissing show. The funny thing is that sometimes schools weren't too happy to have the event covered. They were somewhat embarrassed about having brought a kissing show to their campus, an event that was considered frivolous by many school administrators. Adding to their embarrassment, some newspapers and television stations poked fun at the schools for bringing a kissing show to campus. Their tired old line was: "Do College Students Really Need Instruction in How to Kiss?" These media pundits missed the point that the show functioned primarily as entertainment, and unique entertainment at that.

When I emerged from our rehearsal, leading my eight trained demonstrators up to the stage, I was astonished to see that not one but *two* television stations had arrived. They had installed blinding studio lights to illuminate the stage, and electrical cables snaked along the floor. The room was packed to the gills with attendees too. I looked around nervously, hoping that I wouldn't spot a disgruntled director of student activities or a faculty member who might object to the cameras. Luckily, some schools did appreciate the free coverage that I attracted, and some television producers did a fairly good job reporting the entertaining aspects of the show.

The wonderful thing about having live television coverage at an event like this was how the cameras and lights affected the audience's mood. All the hoopla invariably supercharged the kids with excitement, as if they didn't already have enough energy rushing through their nerves just being at a kissing show. It raised the ante, adding extra punch to all my jokes and extra zing to all the demonstrations. At the same time, it made my volunteers feel like movie stars, and it brought out the ham in most of them. Now they weren't just acting for their classmates, they were performing for the entire city, or sometimes the entire country.

One of the producers came up to me with a cameraman and asked if she could conduct an interview before the performance.

"Could we do it after?" I said. "I'm up against starting time."

"We can't stay all through the show," she explained. "We plan to air the segment on tonight's ten o'clock news, and we need to edit it."

"Okay, then. Interview me!"

She asked a few quick questions, and then we were on. The show went from one high point to the next, and all the time I had two cameras moving around the venue, back and forth in front of the stage, and up and down the aisles. Even though the cameras sometimes obstructed the view, they didn't detract from the audience's enjoyment—just the opposite! Now people in the crowd had to lean left and right to be sure to see all the action, and it was more exciting for them. Plus, every so often the television lights were turned on the audience and the cameras recorded reaction shots of students laughing and clapping, so everyone knew that they too might be on the news that night. I was in seventh heaven, running hither and yon around my volunteers, noticing what a good performance they were delivering, and sensing how much fun the crowd was having. All the excitement was also driving me to my limits, making me almost frenetic in the way I jumped here and there and emoted into my microphone, right up to the end of the show, when I unleashed the car crash—the *almost* car crash.

To my delight, all my revising of the skit paid off. At the moment of near impact, wild screams erupted from the audience. They cheered and laughed, and the new skit became an instant success.

How lucky I was, I thought, to have had that car crash at the Avis lot after all. It had inspired this wonderful result, and the bad had turned out all for the good. That night in my hotel I was like a nutcase switching from channel to channel to catch the news coverage. Yes, there we were! One segment captured all the high-adrenaline feel of the show beautifully, and five or six minutes later the second segment aired on another channel—featuring the car kiss and the near crash! I was unaware that this station had a national affiliation, but when the network editors saw the footage they loved it and quickly squeezed it into their national feed. The kissing show had once again gone viral. Even in those preinternet days an idea could catch on in a heartbeat via television, spreading across America and inspiring other colleges to bring the show to their campus.

A couple of days after I arrived home, Kevin called. "What's going on, Billy? We're getting bombarded with calls about the show."

"Two television stations covered it at Temple," I said. "One of the producers told me yesterday that they sent the segment out to their national affiliate. Maybe that explains it."

"This is as good as doing a national showcase. We've

got six more schools interested, and more calls are coming in all the time."

"I added a car crash too."

"A car crash?"

"I guess I didn't tell you, but I crashed the rental car when I came back from Endicott. I was inspired to add that to the final skit."

Kevin laughed. "Whatever you're doing, keep on doing it."

As the show attracted more publicity, I performed at numerous Florida schools, where students were so liberal that they demanded even wilder skits. In the Sunshine State I was gratified by an overwhelming acceptance of every suggestive skit that I could dream up, and as a result I experimented with additional scenarios—including a vacuum kiss, an androgynous kiss, and a teacher-student kiss—many of which I was prohibited from including in conservative locations like Utah and Oklahoma.

And then in Atlanta and New Orleans I saw things that inspired me to add one of my wildest embellishments yet.

CHAPTER TWENTY

ATLANTA AND NEW ORLEANS

"DO YOU THINK I'M LOSING MY MIND?"

"Why do you ask *that*?"

"I feel like I'm becoming unhinged."

"Unhinged?"

"Mentally unstable."

Cathy was driving me to Rhode Island in the fall of 2000, and I had decided to ask her opinion of my mental state.

One of my favorite philosophers, Arthur Schopenhauer, believed that actors are susceptible to mental illness more than people in any other profession. The reason is that in creating another persona actors begin to lose their own sense of self. I felt the same thing was happening to me. While I was onstage directing the show, I always needed to assume a role. For example, when the couples were preparing for the first kiss, I delivered the line "He leans closer and closer until he can feel the *heat* from her lips on his—and he can't resist her!" Those words were the cue for the boys to kiss the girls. We rehearsed the cue several times to make sure that the boys remembered it.

But you can't simply deliver that line and expect it to

work its magic on an audience. The words themselves are incapable of conveying the full meaning and excitement that a person feels, the sexual attraction and desire that draws them close to the partner they love. The only way to deliver that line properly is for the presenter to thoroughly feel the truth of what he's saying, and I quickly discovered that the audience would not scream with pleasure at that first kiss unless I *personally* felt all the pent-up emotional and sexual attraction that I was talking about.

Yet how could I feel those powerful emotions if the girls on the stage were unknown to me? I had no connection with any of them, I wasn't in love with any of them, and even if I happened to find them attractive, that attraction in and of itself wasn't enough to motivate the line I had to deliver. What I needed was the ability to do what any good Method actor does: I needed to feel the truth in the line by conjuring up an image of a girl that I was really in love with. Now, there was no need for me to mention this mental image to the audience; they didn't have to be privy to what I was thinking. It was for me, and me alone, that I reached for this mental picture, and when I had that image firmly in mind, that image and all the memories associated with it would naturally produce in my heart precisely the right kind of heightened feeling that would make my delivery of the line effective. In short, if I felt it, the audience would feel it too . . . and at the same time they would see four boys leaning in for that first kiss. The combination of my emotionally accurate delivery plus the visual image of the boys kissing the girls for the first time was a surefire way to drive almost any college audience wild.

But now I felt that I was becoming schizophrenic. I

was on the road and far from Judy Youngson, the girl of my dreams, but every day that I did a show I was forced to conjure up her image multiple times so that I could say my lines with the appropriate inflection. I was becoming mentally unhinged, and there was no cure for it. Like many actors, I was on the verge of suffering from a mental illness caused by my work.

You think I'm exaggerating? You find it hard to believe that mental pictures can unhinge a person? Then you've never found yourself in an airplane at thirty thousand feet, flying to a new destination at seven in the morning, sleepless and dozing in and out of consciousness, while simultaneously trying to run through a mental rehearsal of your show and in the process running the image of a close-up pair of lips—soft, glistening, pink, and inviting—over and over through your sleep-deprived brain. It takes you away from reality so effectively that you're literally in another world for the duration of that flight. And when you finally get to your motel you don't even have time to catch a nap before you need to rehearse again in front of the mirror in your room, saying the words aloud and going through the gestures that you'll do that night in front of the crowd. This final rehearsal is vital to a good performance, yet the rehearsal itself contributes to your separation from reality. You hardly have time to comb your hair before you get picked up by students from the entertainment committee and whisked to the school for a sound check.

The mental challenges of doing the kissing show were always exacerbated by my traveling to different parts of the country and having to adapt to local customs, mores, and political climates. Yes, these regional differences could also be stimulating, especially since there were so many lovely cities and people in the South, the Midwest, the West Coast, and the North. When I traveled to Atlanta, for instance, I was always aware that the people in this warm and welcoming metropolis were in some ways more interactive than the New Yorkers I had grown up with as a youth. The first time I walked down the street in Atlanta, a man smiled and said hello as he passed. I turned around to see who he was talking to—but no one was there. Then I realized that people in different parts of the country act differently; in New York when you pass people on the sidewalk, nobody says hello.

In Atlanta the students were more laid-back and less demanding than at Boston schools, but they had the same interest in kissing and the same level of enthusiasm for all the demonstrations. The only difference I noticed occurred when I asked them to do the group kiss. This skit got me the biggest laugh at Cornell, but some southern schools found it a bit over-the-top, and on February 17, 1997, the Georgia State University volunteers in Atlanta did a double take when I broached the subject of an orgy for their show.

"It's not really an orgy," I reassured them. "It's just a make-believe one."

Their mouths fell open and their faces became pale. I had to do a quick mental calculation: Should I drop the skit, or should I talk them into it? I must admit that I have an extraordinary ability to be persuasive. I'm not a con man, however, and I never try to convince demonstrators to do anything that would work against their best interests or that would cause them harm. Still, I believed that the group kiss scenario would be fun for them and for the audience; my concern, though, was to be sensitive and considerate of their feelings. In short, I didn't want to push them past their limits or make them uneasy. Yes, let's move them out of their comfort zone a little and get them to expand their horizons with a group kiss, but let's not make them ashamed of what they're doing. That was my mind-set as I looked at their puzzled faces in the rehearsal room.

I really had nothing to worry about, as you'll see when I tell you what happened *after* the show.

So I explained the scene to them in detail, taking my time to paint an accurate picture of what I expected them to do during the group kiss. "You'll get down on your hands and knees, or stagger around with your hands waving in front of your face, like people groping around a totally dark room where the lights have gone out in a power failure." I didn't mention that I had stolen this scenario from a popular commedia dell'arte *lazzi* where the Italian actors in the traveling troupes would pretend to be unable to see on a moonless night. "Then you'll accidentally bump into the other demonstrators onstage and kiss them on the shoulder or the back of the neck. If the audience is going wild at this point—which they usually do when they see this skit—then I'll give you a signal to move blindly into the crowd. The signal will be when I say, 'The party is spilling into the next room! They're coming toward you to kiss *you*, and you (the audience) are part of the show.' Okay? You're going to be all right doing that?"

They nodded approval, and I then had them rehearse the moves for me right then and there so that I could make sure they would do it right.

When we reached this point in the show at Georgia

State I told the audience that it was dark because there had been a power failure, and their imaginations made it work. The skit went over without a hitch, and the audience appeared to enjoy it, although there wasn't the kind of uproarious reaction like at Cornell. Then after the show, the girl in charge of the event, a young student with a very friendly disposition, took me aside and asked whether I had some extra time or if I had to return to my motel right away.

"I'm free for the rest of the night."

"Good, then you can come with us."

"Where are you going?"

"To a drag show."

"A *drag* show?"

"We have them every year."

"What exactly *is* a drag show?"

"Haven't you been to one before? The guys dress up like women and strip for the audience."

"Are you serious?"

"Come on!"

And I thought *my* show was risqué! I was about to discover that the kissing show was tame compared to what I would see that evening. I really didn't know what to expect, but when she led me into the other auditorium— which was five times the size of the performance space they had booked for the kissing show—I was astounded to see that five times as many students were attending this event than had come to see *The Art of Kissing*. I felt envy and disappointment that my show hadn't attracted as big a crowd, but maybe, I thought, if they had advertised the kissing show more enthusiastically, and if they had scheduled it for this larger venue, perhaps it would have drawn a bigger crowd. At any rate, my jealousy of the success of this late-night event soon passed as we made our way into the middle of the auditorium and took our seats. There were easily five or six hundred students in the place, and they were excited and jabbering with their friends.

Then the house lights dimmed and the master of ceremonies took the stage. He was wearing a big puffy hat.

"Are you ready?" he called into the microphone.

The first performer came onstage to catcalls and whistles of approval: a tall, slender young black man wearing a dark necktie, a white dress shirt, and a white vest and pants. He was clean shaven and had a fedora pulled tight on his head. Red and blue spotlights illuminated him. His eyes were made up with mascara and eyeliner, and his lips were red. He looked like David Bowie. A new song began to play over the loudspeakers, and he strutted across the stage. He was wearing heels, and when his back was to us he looked very seductive. When he removed his fedora, doll-like blond tresses fell over his shoulders, and the illusion was complete. The crowd hollered in excitement.

Then in one quick motion he unbuttoned his vest. Five hundred students roared with glee. The performer removed his vest and fully unbuttoned his shirt. While dancing, he pulled his shirttails out of his pants and turned his back to us. He snapped the shirt off, revealing a tight black corset, and he began gyrating his hips under the red spotlight. A wave of screaming and laughter swept through the hall. It was so loud you couldn't hear yourself talk.

The performer spun around to face us again, and unzipped his pants. Now the noise in the room rose to a crescendo, urging him on—but he needed no further encouragement. He unhesitatingly pulled down his pants and stepped out of them, flinging them aside to reveal lacy underwear. Wearing nothing but undergarments, and looking exactly like a female stripper, he approached first one side of the stage and then the other, casting sultry looks at the audience.

And so it continued for forty-five minutes, one male performer after another stripping to reveal dresses, skirts, hot pants, stockings, and even bikinis. Despite the fact that school administrators might be generally conservative, during their annual drag show students at Georgia State clearly shed all vestiges of Bible Belt mentality. They whistled, cheered, and screamed while young men stripped and strutted across the stage. The crowd's reaction to these performers put me to shame. The kissing show had not drawn as large an audience and had not made the audience scream like this. I wanted this kind of reaction for my show, and I was determined to get it.

How could I incorporate some element of this drag show into *The Art of Kissing*? Was that even possible? Would it work with my performance? And, if so, how could I convince my demonstrators at the various schools to do something so outrageous? I feared that it would be impossible, but I resolved to put my mind on the problem and come up with some kind of response to what I had seen at Georgia State.

Then something curious happened. You might call it synchronicity, the chance occurrence of two things that seem connected but actually have no causal link. In February, for Valentine's Day, I was invited to appear at the on-air studio of Kiss 108, Boston's top-rated hit music station. I had a gig booked that day, and indeed for the preceding and succeeding few days. Valentine's week was one of the most popular times for the kissing show. But they were flexible enough and booked me in the week after Valentine's Day. It was a bitterly cold morning when I emerged from the subway and walked around looking for their studio; there was ice all over the sidewalk so that I almost slipped a few times before I found the entrance to the station.

Inside, I was surprised to be greeted by Sam Rhodes, a young man I knew from my days at WZBC-FM, Boston College's radio station. Sam had reddish hair and a low-key delivery. He'd worked as the engineer at WZBC, and I liked him.

"What are you doing here, Sam?"

"Engineering."

"They invited me to talk about my book."

"Just wait in the green room and the host will be with you in a couple of minutes." The term *green room* turned out to be a euphemism. Sam ushered me into a narrow hallway where two other guests were standing. The on-air program was audible over the speakers in the hall, so we couldn't do much talking.

Then in walked a tall blonde wearing a ballet costume, complete with a short, stiff tutu projecting horizontally from the waist and hip. Why a young woman would wear such an outrageous outfit to a radio station was beyond me, considering no one in the audience would be able to see it. The blonde smiled at me, and I got the shock of my life.

It was actually a guy in drag, but his makeup was so perfect you could hardly tell.

Here again I was going to be competing with a guy

in drag, just like at Georgia State, only this time we'd be competing for audience attention with only our voices and, of course, the reaction of the host and the other on-air personalities. I've done so many radio shows I can't remember what we discussed, but my memory is clear that it was a brief interview of no more than three or four minutes. I also distinctly recall that the host seemed much more interested in talking with the drag queen.

I was vexed because I still hadn't figured out a way to incorporate what I had experienced at Georgia State into my show. My subconscious had been challenged by the question of how to use this role reversal onstage, and I was disappointed that I hadn't come up with a solution.

It just so happened that a third incident added itself to my growing list of encounters with guys in drag, and this led to my breakthrough insight. This time the incident also happened in the Deep South. On November 17, 1997, I was at Tulane University, where the trees are beautiful, the weather warm, and the air sweet and fragrant. William Faulkner and Tennessee Williams had lived in New Orleans, and I was excited to finally be getting a chance to visit this historic literary area. I kept my eyes and ears open as I approached the picturesque campus, and once inside I was met by Larry Greenwood, a premed student in charge of the event. He was short and stocky and one of the friendliest people I ever worked with. Larry was always smiling and telling jokes. I thought he would make an unusual doctor, since most doctors are serious. The show at Tulane went well, and then afterward Larry said, "We're going to take you to dinner, and the school is paying for it, so I hope you accept."

"Gladly!"

"I have a place I think you'll like."

"Really?. . . Where?"

"I want it to be a surprise."

And let me tell you, it *was* a surprise! Larry and one of his associates drove me to a restaurant in downtown New Orleans, and when we arrived he smiled and waved expansively at the tables. I didn't notice anything unusual: there were about twenty tables with white linen tablecloths, and the room was filled with people.

"There's a fifteen-minute wait," the hostess said.

"That's fine," Larry said. Then turning to me, he added, "Right?"

"I have nowhere to go."

We sat at the bar and ordered drinks, and then Larry explained the surprise.

"Bill, all the waiters are guys."

"Hunh?"

"Those so-called waitresses . . ."

My eyes traveled throughout the room again, this time seeing everything in a completely new light. Larry started chuckling.

"Your eyes look like they're bugging out."

"Larry, you don't understand: I was at Georgia State and the kids took me to a drag show, then I went on the radio and there was a drag queen, and now this! These waiters are stunning, but my mind is working overtime because I want to put something like this into my show and I'm trying to figure out how to do it."

"But the show was fine tonight."

"Thank you."

Then he smiled and added, "I thought you would like this place."

Larry had an insightful personality and was sensitive to people. "What kind of doctor do you think I should become?" he asked.

I thought for a moment.

"I don't know, but whatever field you go into, it shouldn't be research in a cold impersonal laboratory. You're a people person."

"Everybody tells me I should be a proctologist." He laughed, and then he added, "Someday when you're old, come to see me and I'll give you a complimentary B-12 shot."

The hostess, who was a young man in drag, finally ushered us to our table, where we were waited on by a drag queen wearing a conservative blouse and slacks. Although Larry didn't suggest a way I could incorporate the drag queens into my performance, the experience of going to that restaurant with him assured me that it would be a good idea for me to take the gender swap to the next level and add it to the show. Over the next few weeks I mulled over some ideas and came up with the concept that I wanted to use.

My next gig was in Florida, and at the start of the rehearsal I told the demonstrators that I was excited to try a new skit that I had never used at any other school. "What I want the boys to do is pretend that they're girls—in their *mind*—while kissing, and try to go through the motions and the experience the way you think a girl would. What will be funny is if a few of you pretend to be extra shy. At the same time, I want the girls to pretend—in their minds—that they're boys, okay?" I could see the girls nodding and getting into it. They understood what I wanted right away. Interestingly, girls have an easier time with this skit than guys. "I want the girls who are pretending mentally to be boys to get aggressive with their dates, okay? Move your hands all over him and don't hold back."

I was a little worried about introducing the skit in the South. After all, I had run into trouble in Alabama with the shower kiss. When we came out of rehearsal there were about 250 students in the venue, and they looked like they were having a good time. Finally we reached the point in the show where I wanted to introduce the new skit, and I started it by saying, "Communication is important in every relationship, and it's vitally important to *understand* your partner. When we're in a relationship, understanding is a critical skill, and one of the best ways to understand your partner is to get into their mind-set as best you can. Probably the best way to do this is the method we're going to demonstrate for you now; while kissing, the guys will pretend—in their minds—that *they* are girls, and the girls are going to mentally imagine that *they* are boys. Okay, folks . . . Go ahead and kiss your partners!"

As soon as the skit started we got oohs and aahs from the crowd. *What's going on here! What's this all about!* In an inspired move, one of the boys raised his foot off the floor, bending his knee as if he were an infatuated teenager. The way he acted appeared totally convincing; without changing his attire, he had completely changed his mannerisms.

Girls shuddered in their seats with amusement at the unexpected sex change, and the playfulness of the other demonstrators contributed to the full effect of the androgynous kiss, as I called it. At school after school, even in the conservative South, this sexual role reversal worked its magic, and I was pleased that I was not only entertaining audiences but also teaching them something useful about how important it is to understand and be sensitive to your partner's perspective and feelings.

CHAPTER TWENTY-ONE

TEXAS AND NEVADA

FOR MANY YEARS I IMAGINED THAT I WAS making a big mistake whenever I did a kissing show in Texas. But if you've ever visited the Lone Star State I think you'll agree that the problem wasn't with me at all. It was caused by the difference in culture from North to South.

I'll readily admit that the kissing show was all about girls: how to approach them, how to talk with them, how to nuzzle up to them, and how to tenderly—and sometimes not so tenderly—plant kisses on their ears, necks, arms, and lips. It was boys doing kisses *to* girls that set the show on fire and got the biggest audience reactions, like in that early kissing show at Stonehill where the boy in red had all the girls screaming with excitement at the way he kissed his partner. She loved it, and the audience loved seeing it.

In Texas in the '90s, I soon learned, audiences didn't like anything too provocative. There was an expectation of gallantry and graciousness toward women—and you were more effective when the guys exuded courtesy and a sense of chivalry.

I directed a show for Valentine's week in Houston, where the average temperature in February is near seventy degrees. The girls showed up for rehearsal in pastel-colored dresses. At first I didn't think they were the volunteers—I thought they were administrators—but the woman running the show, the director of student activities, introduced them to me while I was completing my sound check. The room had been decorated with crimson hearts, red-and-white crepe bunting, and several lavish bouquets of flowers. There were even heart-shaped candies scattered on the chairs. The girls looked like they were going to a prom instead of a kissing show.

How am I going to get them to do the group kiss? I wondered. They acted so prim and proper I was afraid they wouldn't even be able to kiss in public.

The boys, however, seemed like guys at most other schools, except that they treated me with the kind of respect that you rarely receive from college students. I'm used to people from this age group since I've been teaching them for decades, but I went through a complete revolution in my thinking while dealing with these volunteers. I sensed immediately that I would have to treat them with extra care and consideration and make sure that they weren't cast in a bad light during the performance.

As soon as we ensconced ourselves in the rehearsal room I knew that I had my work cut out for me. "This show is all about you," I began. I had picked up this line from Phil Donahue. "Even though I wrote *The Art of Kissing*, the audience doesn't come to see *me* or to hear William Cane talk for an hour—that would be boring. They come to see *you* and to see you demonstrate all the kisses." The girls giggled. They found it funny; not only that, but none of them knew their partners. The student activities office had rounded up single volunteers and had counted on me to match them up. I told the guys to sit on the chairs in the rehearsal room, and I let the girls decide among themselves who they wanted as their partner. This took the burden off my shoulders and gave the girls total control. Eventually four girls were sitting next to four guys, and we had our couples for the show.

The next challenge was getting them to be comfortable with public displays of affection. At some schools the club that invites me to do the event will round up one or two couples who already know each other. They may be dating or even married. Sometimes they're just friends who agree to do the demonstration together. But in this case all the demonstrators were new to each other, and I had a feeling they were going to be shy. In some ways that posed a problem because they might be skittish about kissing, but I decided to use their shyness to my advantage by not pressing them too hard in rehearsal, where they would be kissing each other for the first time; instead, I would go easy on them now and let the excitement of the show hopefully bring out all their exhibitionist tendencies. I knew from past experience that once my volunteers got in front of an audience they usually loosened up and played to the crowd. Sometimes there were exceptions, where a volunteer would get shy in public, but for the most part young people like to show off once they see that the crowd is laughing *with* them, not *at* them during the funny moments that always occur in a kissing performance.

So, for the first kiss in the rehearsal I went easy with them and simply described what they would be doing in the show. I only asked them to touch lips for a quick first kiss in the rehearsal room, and this they readily accomplished, although with more giggles from the girls. The next skit, the shy kiss, was also easy for them. It involved another quick kiss and then a kind of demure glancing around, as if the volunteers were introverted and didn't like to be seen kissing in public.

By the time we went onstage for the show, my reticent demonstrators seemed to have loosened up, but when they sat down and saw that the room was packed, they started to act nervous again. The back of the venue had floor-to-ceiling glass walls and doors that led to the school cafeteria, so once the show began people who were having lunch came up to the windows to see what all the excitement was about. Now and then I had to go up to my volunteers and quietly ask if they were all right. Luckily none of them bolted out of the venue at the last minute, and the entire performance went off without any major complications. In consideration of the fact that the girls were wearing short skirts, I had told them that they didn't need to sit on the boys' laps for the finale during the car kiss, but when we reached that point in the show they seemed to lose their inhibitions and two of the girls put their legs over their partner's and climbed up to kiss them, while the other two simply hugged and kissed the boys from the side. This slight difference between couples added to the entertainment value of the skit, and I was happy for myself and my volunteers when we received a hearty round of applause. The director of student activities even commended us for putting on a fine show after it was over.

If I managed to avoid making a big cultural mistake in Texas, I wasn't so lucky in Nevada. I forget how the show went, but I'll never forget what happened when I took a walk from my motel around ten p.m. in hopes of locating a place to have dinner. I wanted to find something nearby, which is why I didn't take a taxi or bus. The night was warm and dark, and there weren't many streetlights. I found myself in a deserted area near a highway that was about ten miles from the campus where I had directed the show, and I walked about three blocks along an open field searching for a restaurant.

Finally I came to a long white building that looked like it could be a restaurant, although it was dark and hard to see. My vision is so poor at night that I couldn't read the signage over the building. I approached down a cement path, looking for the entrance. The lights were off and I thought that maybe I had come to the back of the restaurant. But there were no paths leading left or right. Puzzled, I decided to try the bell to see if they were still open. If not, I could always ask for directions. But there was no bell, so I knocked on one of the glass panes. It was a wooden door with many little windows that were blocked on the inside by lace curtains.

No reply.

I leaned forward to knock again, but just as I did the door suddenly opened and I lost my balance and fell forward into the arms of a young woman. She had long black hair and was wearing a nightgown. In embarrassment, I straightened up and stammered out an apology.

"No need to apologize," she said.

"Are you open?"

"Do you want to come in?"

She stood aside and beckoned for me to enter, but I stayed where I was. No lights were on inside, and I was confused.

"What kind of restaurant is this?"

"You want food?"

"Yes, I'm looking for a Chinese restaurant."

"We have a Chinese lady, or maybe she's from Thailand, I'm not sure. Is that okay with you?"

"What do you mean?" I said. "Is she the cook?"

"Do you want to see her?"

"No, I don't need to see the chef. But maybe I should just order takeout and bring it to my motel."

"You want her to come to the motel?"

I was getting more confused by the conversation. As my eyes gradually grew accustomed to the dimness, it dawned to me that the restaurant had a rather unusual dress code: the hostess was wearing a semitransparent uniform. I had worked in a number of restaurants myself, but I had never seen anyone dressed like this. Maybe it's just the way they do things in Nevada, I thought.

"That will be an extra charge," the girl said.

"An extra charge for takeout?"

"Yes, for going to the motel."

"But can I see the menu first?"

"Menu?"

"Yes. You know, the selection."

"Oh, certainly. Come inside, and I'll show you six or seven girls so you can select the one you like."

Suddenly it occurred to me that I might have made a wrong turn somewhere.

"Er, what kind of restaurant is this?"

The girl gave me a reproving glance and said, "Oh, you really want a restaurant!" By the time I realized that I was in a different kind of establishment entirely, I had made a complete fool of myself. The young woman put her dark eyes on me and smiled invitingly, but I backed away, too stupefied by what had happened to even ask directions to the nearest restaurant.

Naturally, after I had finally found a place to eat and had returned to my room, my mind was working overtime, and my thoughts all revolved around my experience at the place I had thought was a restaurant. I'm sure you won't be surprised to learn that I was wondering how I could possibly add a prostitute to the kissing show. After putting my mind on this question I eventually came up with an idea that I called the bad boy, bad girl skit. First, the girls would have an opportunity to kiss bad boys, and for this to work the boys would be instructed to act like Hell's Angels and *not* kiss back. I wanted them to act so tough that girls weren't of interest to them. My survey had revealed that many girls have fantasies about being with a bad boy—that is, a boy who doesn't care about them. For example, it can be exciting for young women to be with the James Dean type of loner—a rebel who paradoxically attracts women with his uncaring attitude.

Then the situation would be reversed, and the girls would be instructed to act like uncaring streetwalkers who wouldn't kiss the boys back while the boys attempted to kiss them.

As soon as we introduced this skit it became obvious that the demonstrators enjoyed acting in both scenarios—and audiences in all parts of the country laughed at the antics of the bad boys and bad girls. The kisses that occurred in both sections of the skit contained unexpected surprises and provoked keen interest and curiosity. Little did anyone realize that in a real sense they were laughing at my own folly on the night I accidentally visited a Nevada whorehouse.

CHAPTER TWENTY-TWO

MARYLAND

OVID, MY GREAT TEACHER, TELLS US THAT in the game of love it is vital to make many promises. It's much less important to *keep* those promises. This romantic principle is based on the fact that after you make a promise the surrounding conditions may change; indeed, they are of necessity *going* to change—you can count on *that* if on nothing else in life. And once circumstances change, you can usually finagle your way out of those sugar-coated words. Your partner may even forget what you said.

Armed with this lover's advice from the master Roman poet, I felt confident in making promises to my volunteers that I didn't intend to keep. But it got me into trouble in Maryland.

Before I explain the big mistake I made in the Free State, you should know that many schools fail to do the necessary prep work for the show, including rounding up demonstrators. Such schools usually begged me for help finding volunteers, and when I arrived to do a sound check I would be met with frantic pleas, such as, "We tried but no one volunteered. Can you just pull people out of the audience?"

Yes, I can—but unrehearsed demonstrators resist direction. The unrehearsed volunteer will fight with me and even derive a perverse satisfaction from being obstreperous during the show, thinking they're being funny by refusing to do the shower kiss, the spanking kiss, or even simple skits like the sliding kiss or the first kiss. If these unrehearsed kids haven't heard of a kiss, or if the skit strikes them as too risky, they won't do it. Rehearsal is mandatory, something I knew even from my very first show back in 1991.

Knowing full well the necessity of proper rehearsal, I always sent schools numerous reminders, through fax, email, and phone calls, to urge them to get their own volunteers *before* I arrived. I even gave them practical suggestions regarding how to go about doing this advance work, suggesting that they offer prizes as incentives for students to volunteer, such as free T-shirts or movie passes. In many cases these tactics worked to produce four or five couples who freely volunteered to be in the show, and when I arrived the demonstrators were either already at the venue or they were on their way.

Nevertheless, there were still many schools where the person in charge of the event failed to do their job. Sometimes this failure happened because the student in charge of extracurricular activities had other responsibilities. As all college students do, these club officers had assignments and sometimes other clubs that took up their time. Sometimes they were simply irresponsible and failed to plan ahead. This lackadaisical attitude was one of the biggest frustrations I ran into during my years doing the show, and this was exactly the situation I encountered in the spring of 2003 when I arrived at a particular community college in Maryland.

At these schools where organizers failed to do the preparatory work, the responsibility for rounding up volunteers always devolved upon me. The worst part of it was that it took time to traipse through a campus looking for people, and this reduced the amount of time I had for rehearsal and even prevented me from adequately going over the sound cues beforehand, resulting in a poor technical performance. The rider of my contract specified that the school was required to round up demonstrators before I arrived, but I'm not the only performer who has had trouble with the host of a show failing to carry out the terms of a rider. That's why some bands put clauses in their contracts requiring the organizer of an event to do crazy things, such as provide a bowl of M&M's with all the red candies removed. It's not that they don't like red candy or that they want to be annoying; instead, it's done because if the band arrives and finds that this stipulation hasn't been completed, they're forewarned that other more important measures have also not been followed, including safety measures in a rider relating to electrical grounding, proper security, and the like. The bottom line is that I had to be prepared for those schools that were delinquent in following the conditions of the rider, and I had to help them find volunteers.

You can't imagine how challenging it could be to walk through a college looking for volunteers for a kissing show late at night. Sometimes I would ask one or two of the students from the entertainment committee to accompany me, and we would run through the halls of the classroom buildings at seven o'clock looking for kids wild and crazy enough to jump in at the last minute and do a public kissing demonstration. I would even go through the library trying to get students to stop studying and volunteer to be in the show. Other times we would walk through the dormitories, knocking on doors, disturbing people in the privacy of their residences, asking them to drop everything at a moment's notice and come to rehearsal. And I was perfectly aware that with each passing minute that I spent in this activity, I was taking time away from the important rehearsal. When it took me longer than usual to get volunteers, I wound up with only fifteen or twenty minutes to rehearse. Truncated rehearsals like that were a ticket to disaster.

Through similar experiences at many schools, I became adept at spotting students who might be good volunteers, and I could often sense who would be an effective actor and who would be problematic just by talking with them for a few seconds. I got into the habit of going up to people and opening the conversation by saying: "Hi, I want you to say *yes*!"

If they replied unhesitatingly with an enthusiastic "Yes!" and a smile, it suggested that they were friendly, impulsive, and daring—a perfect temperament to shine in the kissing show.

Once they said "Yes," I would say, "Thank you! Your college also thanks you because you said yes to being in a kissing show."

If they were still smiling and enthusiastic, they were my ideal volunteer. Usually, however, a student would not reply with the yes I needed to hear, and I would immediately pass them by and walk up to the next prospect. I didn't need people who thought too much or who weren't spontaneous.

Another effective technique that I used was offering

prizes to volunteers. I would promise the moon if I had to, simply to get people to say that they'd come with me immediately, drop all their other plans, and spend an hour in rehearsal and then another hour doing the show. At first I tried offering prizes that the student activities committee really had available, and I would ask the kids who brought me to campus if they had any giveaway items that we could use to lure demonstrators into the show. Often the things they had were of little value, such as T-shirts, baseball caps, and free movie passes. Nevertheless, even these small incentives worked like charms. One of the reasons that a small incentive can motivate a college student is that it makes the volunteer appear less desperate to his friends; in other words, if a potential volunteer's pals are nearby when they're asked to volunteer, they won't appear to be volunteering in order to have an erotic experience; they can instead appear to be interested in the prizes being offered.

Some of the most effective recruiting took place when I could enter the college dining room and approach a table with a bunch of boys and ask for volunteers. If one of the boys seemed even mildly interested, his other friends would often egg him on, hoping to see him do something silly onstage. Or if one boy had the courage to volunteer, then others might volunteer at the same time, joining under peer pressure. Usually they would ask me if the girls were pretty, and even if I didn't have any female volunteers yet, I would say things like: "You won't believe how hot they are!" I used the same tactics at tables where girls were sitting. They were usually shier about volunteering—but not always. Sometimes theatrical types jumped at the opportunity to be onstage, and if one girl volunteered it was much more likely that some of her girlfriends would also come to rehearsal.

When boys and girls were together at a table, the dynamic changed yet again—sometimes they were couples and they could volunteer together. Or if they weren't already dating, they might be friends, in which case there was a chance that there might already be a simmering attraction between them just waiting for a spark to ignite it, and these couples often found the idea of appearing in a kissing demonstration exciting. Whenever I sensed that those dynamics were at work, I would play upon their unconscious desires and do my utmost to motivate them to join the party.

Unfortunately, at this particular school I was having no luck finding volunteers, and the clock was ticking. When I had only half an hour before showtime, I came across two girls sitting outside the library. One was clearly the leader, and the other seemed to be her sidekick the way she let her friend do all the talking and make all the decisions.

"Say yes to me!" I said.

Neither girl said anything.

I should have moved on, but by this time I was desperate so I didn't leave them. I now had only twenty-five minutes to curtain, and as a result I resorted to Ovid's old standby, making promises I couldn't keep.

"I'll give you tuition remission if you volunteer."

"Volunteer for what?"

"A kissing show."

I had to explain what a kissing show was. I didn't want to scare them off, so I told another white lie, one I often used to entice demonstrators.

"You don't even have to kiss the boy. Just make believe."

"And you'll pay my tuition?"

"The student activities board will," I lied.

Slowly but surely, both girls got up and said they'd do it. I was elated, and I led them back to the venue. Now we had a mere twenty minutes remaining before the curtain went up, and I had to rush through rehearsal. It never struck me as worrisome that the confident girl didn't once touch her lips to the boy she was rehearsing with; I thought she was saving all her best moves for the show.

But when we went on in front of about two hundred people, I had four couples and only three of them actually kissed. The so-called confident girl faked each and every demonstration, but at least she was onstage and she was making believe—that is, leaning close—for the different kissing scenarios. Though she was not an enthusiastic volunteer, her confident attitude seemed to make up for a lack of real kissing, and the show went over well enough with the audience and got a lot of laughs and applause, right up to the final skit. So I thought that I had a success on my hands and that I had salvaged an untenable situation by finding these demonstrators.

But after the audience had left the auditorium, the confident girl approached me and said: "Where's our tuition refund?"

"We'll go to the student activities office," I said. "Just let me get my props together."

She and her girlfriend looked impatient.

"Okay," I said. "Let's go right now."

They accompanied me downstairs to the student activities office, but the entertainment committee officer didn't have anything except T-shirts.

"What about my tuition?" the confident girl said.

"I'm sorry," I said. "They can't provide it."

She set her jaw and her eyes became slits.

"You promised!"

"But that promise was so ridiculous," I said, "you *couldn't* really have believed it."

"I did the show because of it."

"Well, you got to kiss a boy, didn't you?"

"Do you think I liked doing that? I never even touched my lips to his. Now I want my money."

"Listen, I don't have it."

The two girls started to become aggressive. I thought this might be a good time to slip out of the room, but they stood barring my way and they looked like they wanted to fight. Without warning, I pulled a quick end run on them and dashed down the hall to the security office to request assistance.

"You got us in a lot of trouble," Kevin said to me the next day. He had called after receiving a report from the school.

"But Kevin, those kids were threatening me physically."

"The director of student activities is a big NACA head. She's going to make life difficult for us. She said the show went well, but that your actions afterward, and promising tuition remission, were unacceptable. Don't you realize that she's going to vote against you every time we try to get another showcase? This is going to hurt us, and it might impact our other acts, I don't know."

My lecture agents were furious because this fiasco would damage their reputation and possibly even reduce their income. I vowed that I would never again offer tuition remission to my demonstrators. But even to this

day I don't regret what happened. It taught me the lesson
that some people will believe what they want to hear, no
matter how implausible. The only regret I have is how
the circumstances caused my agents grief. In the future
I would make sure the student activities office had real
prizes to offer volunteers.

CHAPTER TWENTY-THREE

SAN DIEGO AND SALT LAKE CITY

PEOPLE NEVER CEASE TO AMAZE ME. WHEN I traveled to San Diego, one director of student activities was an extremely friendly guy who always had a five o'clock shadow, even when he picked me up at the airport in the early afternoon. The first time I met him he was with a girl from the student activities committee. I thought the two were simply friends, but when they took me into the airport cafeteria to buy me lunch, the director sat so close to his associate that their arms touched.

I mention this curious observation for one simple reason: it fits into a pattern of activity that I began to notice at other schools too.

In Salt Lake City one director of student activities was an attractive thirty-year-old divorcée. The kissing show was held in a tricky venue for a performer, right in the hallway of the student union. The reason they placed me there was that they didn't want to go through the trouble of advertising the show properly and developing an audience for it. Instead, they reasoned that if they situated the performance in front of the foot traffic in the student union, it would slow people down and draw them to the event. I didn't let such matters bother me. I could perform anywhere.

This young woman left me alone to set up my chairs and props, and as she was walking away she mentioned that she would send the student in charge of the event to help with whatever else I needed. Before long a young man arrived, introduced himself as Douglas, and offered to assist me in setting up the venue. He had sandy hair and looked like John Denver, except that he didn't wear glasses. But after two minutes he stopped what he was doing and said, "Did Annie say anything?"

"What do you mean?"

"Er . . . like . . . did she say she was coming back?"

"No, I don't think so."

As soon as I said that, my little helper lost all interest in assisting me. He made some excuse and left the venue. I didn't think anything about it until much later, as I'll explain in a moment.

When my demonstrators arrived, I took them into a nearby private rehearsal space and then, after about forty-five minutes, we returned to the performance area. Nobody was there to see the show except a few kids from the student activities office. I was disappointed. These club members were wearing lemon-yellow T-shirts and seemed friendly enough, but you always want to attract more of an audience, if only to justify the fact that the school spent money to host the event. Just as I was about to begin, Annie breezed into the hallway, followed by Douglas. The director of student activities smiled and said that once I started talking it would attract a larger crowd. Then she disappeared back down the hallway toward her office, with Douglas close at her heels.

I began my presentation, speaking into the microphone, and sure enough, as she had predicted, students who were walking by stopped to linger and listen, and before long about twenty-five people were sitting on folding chairs watching the performance. I thought I did a decent job at a school where there was almost no advance preparation.

It amazed me how the director of student activities never complained or even commented on the low turnout. None of the students from the committee had anything negative to say either. Everyone seemed to think this meager attendance was perfectly fine, and that was okay with me; if they were happy, I was happy. And as Kevin had told me more than once, as long as I did the show and didn't antagonize anyone, I would get paid no matter how few people showed up.

The director of student activities had mentioned before the show that she would be the person driving me back to my motel, and I was glad when she returned to get me. Sometimes there is confusion at schools and you can wait an hour for your ride, but things were moving along nicely here.

"Would you like to get lunch?" she asked. "I haven't had anything yet this afternoon, and the school has budgeted a meal for you."

"Sounds great."

She drove to a restaurant at the top of a hill, and we sat in a booth and ordered sandwiches and iced tea. I was exhausted but glad to be able to relax and chat with this young woman and possibly receive some feedback about my performance. She didn't seem interested in providing much feedback, however, so I didn't press her on the issue. Her nonchalance reinforced my belief that some schools don't expect a big turnout at an event, and they're just as happy with a small audience. So I was feeling rather content, when she said something that turned the conversation in an unexpected direction.

"What do you think about the members of the student activities committee?" she asked. "Were they helpful to you?"

"Yes, very," I lied.

"Even Douglas?"

I didn't want to mention how he had abruptly left me in the middle of the setup. I had no reason to complain at that point, since everything had worked out fine. So I said, "He was very helpful."

She paused momentarily and fixed her dark eyes on me.

"Douglas has been acting inappropriately with me," she continued.

This statement took me by surprise.

"Really?"

"I mean he treats me as if I was . . . a student."

"Is that so?"

I didn't know where she was going with this conversation, so I just let her talk.

"He thinks he can treat me like one of his classmates."

"How so?"

"He's trying to date me."

"You're kidding."

"Do you know what he said to me the other day? He said, 'Annie, let's go out together and we can pretend it's a date.' I told him that he couldn't talk to me that way and that I didn't date students. But he's . . . well, frankly, he's infatuated with me. And I don't know how to handle it."

Suddenly I felt I understood what she was talking

about, and I remembered how he had left me when he learned that Annie was back in her office. It was clear that Douglas had preferred to be with her than to help set up the show. But he seemed like a harmless enough young man, and I didn't think what he was doing was so terribly wrong. Indeed, now I understood that there was a way for this young woman to take advantage of his interest and turn it in a good direction.

"First, I have to ask if you want to date him."

"Oh, heavens no. He's . . . he's too young."

"Okay, then you have to realize that there's a way to deal with this situation that can help him."

"There is?"

"Teachers experience this reaction from students all the time: they seem to fall in love with you, but it's only transference. You know, like Freud talked about."

"What's transference?"

I guess she was never much into psychology, so I told her how Freud had discovered that his patients developed an emotional attachment to him, and that he often felt an equal countertransference, or emotional attachment, toward them, especially toward female patients. Both he and Carl Jung, as well as a number of other therapists at the outset of psychoanalysis, had affairs with their patients. It's a matter of historical record that Jung built a tower at Bollingen where he had secret rendezvous with one of his patients, Toni Wolff.

While I was explaining these things, the woman's face began to change color until it became nearly as red as her dress.

"Do you mean to tell me," she said, "that you have relationships with your students?"

"I'll say this much," I said. "They develop feelings for me, and I use it the same way Freud did—to help them."

"To *help* them?"

"Yes, of course. If you notice that a student is interested in you, even flirting actively with you, what you can do is use that emotional connection to draw closer to this young man and find out more about his life, and in that way you can encourage him to open up and talk more freely than most students would. Then you can see if he needs help or guidance with different areas of his life; for example, you can recommend books and movies for him, and you can become like a mentor or a parent substitute. Transference can work perfectly effectively in a friendly relationship as well. You need to stop being afraid of his flirtation; in fact, if you allow it to continue, you may be able to guide him more effectively during the formative years of his life."

Annie sat back in her seat and regarded me carefully under the leaden droop of her eyelids.

"Oh, thank you," she said. "I never in a million years would have thought of approaching it in this particular way."

I finished my iced tea, and then she drove me to my hotel, and we didn't discuss the matter further.

At other schools too I started to see a similar pattern emerging: there would be a close working relationship between the director of student activities and the students, and sometimes a relationship seemed to be developing that was more than friendship. These observations got me thinking about the student-staff relationship in a new way.

Then one day in the summer of 2000 Cathy came to

visit me, and she told me that her boyfriend was becoming jealous and thought that there was something going on between us. "I drive you to events, I went to Nashville with you, and I sleep over at your apartment and you sleep at mine sometimes, and I'm always picking you up at the airport, and when I tell him all the things I'm doing with you—including that MTV shoot—he gets worried." She was referring to the film project that we submitted to MTV featuring her considerable acting talents.

I smiled and stood up. She was beaming at me in the sunlight slanting through my windows.

"Maybe we should give him something to worry about," I joked.

She laughed and said, "Professor, you should add a student-teacher kiss to the show."

That remark, together with the way I had seen students interacting with their directors of student activities, convinced me that a student-teacher skit might be effective, provided it was handled with a light and humorous approach. I immediately got to work on it, and once I had the routine worked out on paper, I decided to try it at the next school. Naturally I was a little nervous about it since it was new and slightly risqué. But when I added it to the rehearsal, my demonstrators started laughing, and I had a hunch that I was onto something good. When we reached that part of the show, I introduced it like this:

"Now we're going to share a deep, dark fantasy that many college students experience, and maybe some of you have experienced it too. The girl is sitting in class, and the bell rings and all the other students leave. She is holding a notebook on her lap, and she asks the professor a question."

At this point the guy approaches from behind and looks over the girl's shoulder, down at the book she's holding. I continue to paint the scene.

"Little does the professor know that this young woman is infatuated with him and that she has already taken three of his classes. The professor happens to be near-sighted, and he can't see her notebook clearly, so he has to lean *down—down—down*."

Each time I say the word *down* the boys lean farther down until their noses touch the books.

"He's so close," I continue, "and she's so excited . . . and then he turns and looks at her—"

In unison, all the professors snap their heads around from the books and gaze up into the girls' eyes.

"—and her fantasy becomes a *reality* as he kisses her."

The boys now kiss the girls, and in response the girls drop their notebooks and raise their hands to caress their partner's head and run their fingers through his hair.

Of course the audience goes wild.

"She's so excited . . . she goes *straight* to heaven."

They're still kissing—

"And he . . . he goes straight to *jail*!"

This line kills them. They laugh out all their pent-up anticipation, and I know I've hit a sensitive nerve, one that Freud uncovered years ago in Vienna, one that I've seen operating many times on the college lecture circuit, and one that my muse reminded me about with her suggestion to try a teacher-student kiss.

CHAPTER TWENTY-FOUR

THE DENTIST SKIT

I DIDN'T USUALLY BOOK GIGS IN THE SUMMER, so it was a good time to relax and take care of things I'd put off during the school year. One August afternoon I dragged myself into the Boston University Dental Health Center for a long overdue checkup. A 1997 *Reader's Digest* article had convinced me that dental schools are better than commercial dentists because they're unlikely to recommend unnecessary procedures. But I never anticipated that this visit would inspire one of my most successful kissing skits.

Subdued lighting and oak wall panels greeted me inside. The receptionist explained that a dental student would be with me shortly.

A dental student? No wonder the prices were so low! The article had implied that professors supervised clinicians at these schools, but it looked like I had been assigned to an unsupervised student. I threw myself onto a leather sofa in the vacant waiting room and considered leaving. Why should I trust myself to a dental student, after all? What if this neophyte made some hideous mistake while doing a procedure? Within five minutes I had worked myself up into a tizzy. I was getting ready to walk out the door when a thin redhead breezed into the room and parked herself directly in front of me. She was about twenty-five and was wearing a white lab coat.

"Hi, there."

Hi, there, indeed! And in a deep southern accent too. Who in God's name is *this*, I'm wondering.

"My name is Claudia. I'm a fourth-year student, and I'll be helping you today."

So, *this* was my dentist! She invited me to follow her into the operatory. Dear reader, I didn't walk into the examining room behind her, I floated. No question about it, things had changed for the better in a profoundly agreeable way.

She leaned over and began her examination. And while she was examining me, I tried to think of anything under the sun that would get my mind off what was happening in that office. I tried thinking about baseball, wrestling, books, atomic physics, plasma cosmology, Galileo, space exploration, science fiction, Eugene Ionesco, Samuel Beckett, Charles Dickens—all interests of mine—but none of this helped in the slightest. In fact, the more I attempted to push my mind in different directions with random thoughts, the more insistently my feeble brain kept coming back to my present circumstances in that plush examining chair.

My dentist—and I admit that I started thinking of her as my dentist right away—was chatting with me as she worked, forcing me to focus on her. It was small talk of the most mundane nature, but I felt compelled to keep up my end of the conversation even though it was a near impossibility while her fingers and the tools of her trade impeded my efforts. I simply could not concentrate. For some reason I found myself irresistibly distracted by everything she was doing.

I was suddenly hoping she would find innumerable problems to fix so that I would have to come back many times and let her bestow her ministrations upon me. Her fingers tinkered with my molars and bicuspids, and I was embarrassed to find myself becoming mesmerized. I tried to stop myself from imagining sinking my teeth into the side of her neck and giving her a biting kiss.

We were in such close proximity that I could feel the heat from her face on mine, and I could smell the fragrance of clove rising off her dental instruments. To make a long story short, I went back for three appointments with this student, and every time I returned she worked the same mysterious chemistry on my nervous system, hovering over me, examining my mouth with probes and mirrors, and enveloping me in intoxicating antiseptic aromas.

Before each appointment I would lie abed and fight with myself about whether I should even go back to her, knowing full well that each time she led me into that little dental office I would find myself surrounded by sights and sensations I had no power to control, and most of all no power to stop—unless I did the unthinkable and jumped out of that chair and dashed from the room. My ambivalence was made more acute when, after my three allotted visits, she finally graduated, and alas! was no more to be seen.

Naturally I discussed my mental state with my driver, Cathy. She gave me an inscrutable smile and regarded me with amused eyes. She claimed she understood what she embarrassingly called my infatuation with this dental student. More than this, she *approved* of it. And why was she so understanding? Well, she confessed that she had experienced her own little infatuation with *her* doctor. So she understood perfectly my reaction to my dentist. After all, my dentist had been a young woman, and she had been quite close to me and, what's more, she had been inadvertently stimulating a sensitive area of my mouth. As I'm fond of explaining to my audiences, the mouth has more nerve endings than any other part of the body. It wasn't surprising, Cathy freely acknowledged, that I should find myself unintentionally attracted to this young woman.

I mulled over Cathy's response for some days, until I had to go on the road again. This time I was traveling to a small college in Ohio. When I arrived at the venue a new idea popped into my mind. I approached the director of student activities, a young woman with extremely curly hair.

"Can you bring me four white lab coats?"

Her eyes bugged out, and the halo of ringlets on her head seemed to vibrate with accusatory menace.

"Lab coats?"

Oh, but friends, I had no intention of backing down.

"I know it wasn't in the rider," I said, "but either lab coats or chef's jackets, which might be available from the cafeteria staff. I have an idea for a new skit that I've never done before, and I'm excited about it. I'm sure it will liven up the show."

Student activities offices always had access to lab coats from chemistry and biology students, as well as white jackets from the cafeteria, so I could usually have this costume on hand for the demonstration. But I soon started carrying three lab coats with me when I traveled, just in case.

When I preset the show I arranged a line of chairs onstage facing the audience. Each couple's chairs were touching, and I left a space of two feet between each couple. I also draped a lab coat over the back of every other chair. This was all the audience saw when they entered the venue: chairs and lab coats. *What's it all about?* They came in and looked for a place to sit, and then they gawked at the stage and began to wonder . . . *What's going to happen? What am I going to see in this show?* By the time I was introduced their imaginations were working overtime and they were ready for anything.

The lab coat was of course for the new dentist skit that I had dreamed up in response to my visits to that dental student. Twenty minutes into the show I set the scene.

"Some people practice a kiss by kissing their pillow. Some people kiss a doorknob—"

This got a laugh.

"—because it's smooth," I explained. "But without doubt the best way to practice . . . *is to use your imagination.*"

The guys onstage stood and donned their lab coats, buttoning them up. All of this had been carefully rehearsed so that they got the lab coats on quickly.

"There she is—in her dentist's office," I explained. The crowd leaned forward and regarded the seated girls with heightened appreciation. So *that's* where she was! *The dentist's office! Why . . . oh, why was there a dentist's office in a kissing show?* On an unconscious level I had stirred up curiosity as well as anxiety (which would be relieved shortly with extraordinary bouts of laughter, almost hysterical laughter), and—most important of all—I had awakened buried memories of the kind of oral contact that always accompanies a visit to the dentist. Earlier in the show I had carefully prepared the audience for this moment by planting the idea that kissing involves oral pleasure. Freud tells us as much, I had reminded them: we all pass through the oral stage in our developmental years. And I had quoted Adam Phillips, a British psychiatrist, who said, "Kissing involves some of the pleasures of eating in the absence of nourishment." Now it was time for the payoff—the big payoff. Calmly and serenely I informed them, "Her dentist is a good-looking guy. And he comes in with that little mirror . . ."

At this cue the boys produced dental mirrors, which I had distributed to them during rehearsal.

"And he holds the mirror over her mouth and begins to examine her."

In rehearsal I had pointedly instructed the young men to put their left hand on the girl's left shoulder, and I now reminded them of this instruction, talking them through the skit as it happened in real time:

"He puts his left hand on her left shoulder and looks into her mouth . . . and she's thinking—"

Like a novelist, I moved right into the girl's mind. And, having no choice, the audience accompanied me into her subconscious. *Wheeeeeeee!* I also physically moved into the action by sitting in one of the vacant chairs onstage (since all the boys were standing, there was one vacant chair in each couple). I tried to select a couple with an attractive guy playing dentist.

"She's thinking, *He looks good . . . He smells good . . . He has a good practice . . . I wonder what it would be like to kiss him!*"

I sprang to my feet and moved to another couple,

this time selecting one with an attractive girl playing the patient. The boys were standing, looking down at the girls. I positioned myself behind one of the boys and continued my narration, delving into *his* mind now.

"And the dentist is thinking, *Look at that mouth . . . Look at those teeth . . . Look at this view!*"

I was rewarded with giggles and guffaws from the audience.

Then I stepped into the house and moved to the back of the venue. The audience couldn't see me now—all they could see were the couples onstage. I was behind the audience, talking into the microphone.

"He begins to massage her arm." As I narrated it, the boys did it. "She starts to have a fantasy—about her dentist. She's being orally stimulated, and he holds the mirror out at a ninety-degree angle . . ." The boys held their mirrors away from the girls. "And he leans down . . . closer and closer . . . until there she is—*kissing . . . her fantasy dentist!*"

The boys leaned down and kissed the girls. In rehearsal, I had instructed the girls to throw their arms around their partner's neck. The dentists were instructed to kiss their patients while standing and to not let her knock them off balance for at least ten or fifteen seconds. The girls were given a contrary direction to attempt, with all their might, to pull the dentists down by the neck and tackle them to the floor. Meanwhile I was narrating what was happening, so the audience could simultaneously see the action and hear it described as the dentists and patients struggled.

"He's your *fantasy* dentist! . . . *Claim him! . . . Make him yours!*"

By this time most of the girls had managed to pull their dentist off balance. The boys attempted to maintain their ridiculous stance, with the little mirrors held out to the side and one hand on the girl's shoulder. They were off balance to start with, and one by one the dentists fell to the floor or onto their partners, at which point the girls—who had been instructed never to let go of their dentist during this scenario—followed the boys down to the floor, tackling them and kissing them all the way.

I ran back to the stage and jumped onto the last vacant chair, leapfrogging across them and speaking wildly into the microphone while thunderous music blared from the speakers: *"He's yours, yours, yours! . . . Rip his clothes off! . . . You want another appointment! . . . Have your way with him! . . . You want to marry your dentist!"*

And the girls were doing just that—ripping off lab coats, kissing the guys, mounting them, and sending the crowd into convulsions of laughter. All the audience's bottled-up anxiety about visiting the dentist now got released. There were no drills, no cavities, no pain—it was all pleasure, mercifully and blissfully presented in one of the most rousing spectacles of onstage craziness they'd ever witnessed. They cried, they actually cried tears of pleasure to see the dentist skit.

CHAPTER TWENTY-FIVE

THE FRENCH KISS

"I *CAN'T* BE THERE."

"Why not?"

"I'm going to Las Vegas."

"Las Vegas?"

"I need a vacation."

"But—"

"No ifs, ands, or buts. I'm *going*."

"But who's going to help me?"

I was on the phone with Cathy, and it was annoying me that she was canceling her promise to help direct my new kissing project.

"Are you kidding?" she said. "Can't you handle it yourself?"

"No, I expect too many people."

She was deserting me just when I thought I had a brilliant project to capture the attention of even more people. It was the summer of 2000 and I had recently been nominated Lecture Entertainer of the Year by the National Association for Campus Activities. My show had reached a zenith of popularity on the college lecture circuit. But I was never satisfied, and I now wanted to reach out to an even younger audience. In fact, I had been furiously trying to think of something that could keep young people interested in my work, and I had hit upon the idea of making a DVD of *The Art of Kissing*. I figured Cathy would be intrigued by the prospect of appearing in a movie, and I would be inspired by her presence while directing the project. We would develop the story together, audition actors, and get things rolling. But now she was backing out at the last minute and I was left with no assistant director.

"When are you leaving?"

"Saturday."

As soon as I got off the phone I started thinking. What could I do between now and Saturday to get her to change her mind? I needed to get her to come to the audition—that was it!

I had arranged many auditions, and it was a breeze for me to organize another one for my new project. It was a lot of work, but it wasn't particularly difficult. I knew exactly how to set it up, and I went about it like a madman, putting my plan into place. First, I rented a bar in downtown Boston. It had a wood-paneled basement that would be ideal for auditioning actors.

Then I placed an ad for performers. In order to motivate them to show up, I promised to pay $355 an hour, the same amount I paid Cathy to drive me to shows. It was an outrageously high rate of pay. No one advertises such an exorbitant fee for actors, but I did it because I wanted a lot of people to audition, and as a result my phone was ringing off the hook.

"I want to be in the movie."

"Is that a misprint about $355 an hour?"

"When can I come in?"

"Can I audition with my friend?"

I had advertised that I wanted couples for a kissing film, and I also invited individuals to audition if they were willing to be matched up with other actors for kissing demonstrations. The purpose of the project was to put all thirty kisses from *The Art of Kissing* onscreen so viewers wouldn't have to read the book.

"Why did you make this DVD?" reporters asked me in the months following the project.

"The reason I made it is simple. Even though I wrote an entertaining and informative book, unfortunately some people don't like to read. A lot of kids have their eyes glued to the television all day long. That's what they respond to. Video. They contact me all the time asking, 'How do I do a first kiss?' and 'Do I really have to use my tongue for a french kiss?' How many times have I answered these questions? Thousands! The answers are in my book, of course, but do people read it? Maybe they do, but they never seem to understand. The reading comprehension rate is deplorable today. These young people can't even figure out that a french kiss by definition involves the tongue. So I decided to make a movie that answers all their questions."

That's what I told reporters.

But the truth was quite different. I didn't make the DVD of my book to answer anybody's questions. I didn't do it to help the world understand kissing better. I did it for one reason and one reason alone: to satisfy my obsessive need to direct. I had directed my younger siblings in dramas, my high school friends in plays, actors at the Boston Arts Group, and of course hundreds of demonstrators in the kissing shows. So it's no wonder that I felt an almost irresistible compulsion to direct a movie version of my book.

The fact that Cathy was planning to leave town for the summer didn't stop me either. I sent her a notice about the audition anyway. I told her that I needed her assistance at the bar where I would be auditioning hundreds of actors. But the truth is that I didn't really need her: she had no special background that qualified her to work at auditions, she had little or no experience with theatrical productions, and she was abrupt and autocratic when dealing with people. Her presence at the audition wouldn't help the actors one bit; it would actually make the whole process more difficult, and she would probably get in the way. I knew she wouldn't help me run the process, but I still wanted her there.

She was very well-read, especially in American history and ancient Greek drama, and over the past two years, almost like a dramaturge, she had given me useful feedback on a play about Sigmund Freud that I was writing. I thought she could be a dialogue coach for this project. And while her strong point wasn't exactly tactfulness, she did have intuition that sometimes enabled me to see cast and crew members in a new light. For instance, after our MTV shoot she mentioned that the director of photography had a babyish voice and had struck her as being childish.

I also wanted her to be one of the actors in this project. But ironically it was probably her intractableness that made me want her there more than anything else. She would fight and resist like a wild horse, rejecting ideas and suggestions with a petulant toss of her hair or a dismissive hand gesture. At an audition earlier that year for another film project, Jessica and Cathy had both been production assistants, and Jessica complained to me about the way Cathy contemptuously expressed displeasure with a suggestion she had made. But when Cathy finally came around to a director's way of thinking, she was unmatched in her ability to follow his lead.

I felt stimulated by the challenge of working with her, and our personalities seemed to mesh in a playful tug-of-war dance for control. I think it's fair to say that everything about her inspired me. So I went ahead and told her that I needed her and that she would be an indispensable assistant for me.

But at the same time I arranged it so that I had other assistants who could actually help me. I secured the services of a few production assistants who had experience working on film projects, and I arranged for two camera operators to record the auditions. Then I sat back and waited. I had close to 150 people lined up to come to the basement of this bar on Winter Street for the audition.

Once the audition started I became totally involved in doing what I had to do. There were hundreds of details I had to oversee. It was impossible to even keep in mind that Cathy might show up. I had two folding tables in the audition area in the basement, and I was sitting beside a lovely young woman named Donna Wong, who had worked as a model and was now my assistant director. She was actually doing a fantastic job. If only Cathy could act like her! But Cathy's personality was totally opposite Donna's. My assistant director was a good listener, she was calm, and she jumped to carry out my slightest wishes. She was even able to anticipate my needs during the audition—such as putting up a sign on the door, getting coffee for my production assistants, and coordinating the camera operators. Cathy, on the other hand, was a rather poor listener, was intensely anxious, and almost never thought about my needs. So why was I so eager to have her there? The answer is quite simple. It may sound incomprehensible to a businessperson, but I freely admit that I'm *not* a businessperson, not by a long shot; indeed, every business venture I've ever had has failed. The only thing I'm good at is coming up with crazy ideas like this movie project. Naturally a creative person needs inspiration. Despite the fact that Cathy had no talent for theatrical preproduction, I was convinced that her presence would inspire me to do my best work. If I could impress her with the actors I selected or the dialogue I wrote, then I knew my wider audience would react favorably to my material too. She was the most incomparable muse I had ever met, and if she showed up at the audition, I knew I would work better and be more productive.

So there I was, sitting next to my amazingly empathetic assistant, and actors were pouring into the place. It looked like Grand Central upstairs where people were waiting. Then, one by one, and two by two, the auditioners were sent down to the staging area where they performed their auditions for me.

After this had been going on for an hour and I had seen more than thirty actors, I heard someone on the stairs. No one was supposed to come down those stairs unless my production assistants sent them to me. So I looked up, surprised. And I saw one blonde leg . . . and then another . . . and then a pair of white shorts . . . and then a bare midriff, smooth and tanned, and my pulse started to skyrocket because I knew who it was—it was her!

Yes, Cathy strolled into the room.

It was like a shock to my heart, and I couldn't concentrate. She was standing at my side and I could smell the familiar woodsy perfume. Her hair was long and loose. She was wearing a white cotton halter top. I wanted to drop everything and talk with her. But I couldn't. I had to focus on what I was doing.

She stood by my side, watching an older couple audition.

"Let's see a kiss," I said.

They kissed.

"Lean the girl back and kiss her."

They had trouble setting it up.

"Like in *Gone With the Wind*," I suggested. "Take her in your arms and lean her back."

The guy did it and then they were finished. After they departed Cathy leaned down and told me, in a stage whisper, "You can't use them. They're not good-looking enough. Remember, this DVD is for a *national* audience. You have to use only the best."

I could tell that she wasn't exactly happy to see Donna sitting by my side, but she acted nonchalant and said, "She's good."

"Who?"

"Your assistant."

"Oh, really?"

"Yes."

I knew that she was right, but I also sensed that she was slightly jealous.

She didn't stay long, maybe twenty minutes. But it was

enough to supercharge my nervous system. I didn't drink coffee at the time, but I knew what coffee felt like. Seeing her was like having two cups of coffee. My heart was racing for the next few hours. I auditioned people like a fiend, one after the other in quick succession. I became superorganized and efficient because I wanted to be finished with it. I wanted to get out of there. I couldn't stand being there anymore because I wanted to calm down.

I packed up, took my videos and put them in my suitcase, and thanked Donna. I expected that she would be helping me with the shoot, which I planned to begin in two weeks. I had to get a few locations nailed down first and arrange to have my hair and makeup artists ready. And I needed a props man.

On the taxi ride back to my luxury apartment in the same building where Faye Dunaway used to live in the Prudential Center, I was struck with an idea. The idea was calculated to get millions of people interested in my work again. I suddenly knew how to arrest the attention of the public, teenagers, and anyone who might be a reader of my book and a potential purchaser of this DVD. It seemed clear to me that I could do it with my next original idea.

This is what I was thinking. While I was being driven home I visualized in my mind's eye that I was in a huge mouth.

Yes, that was it!

A mouth. A cavernous mouth—with two monstrous tongues.

The tongues, naturally, were french kissing. So there we were in a huge mouth, and two tongues were going at it, just like in any french kiss, with one exception . . . The way I was going to get the public interested in me again is that I was going to be inside that huge mouth with those two huge tongues *while the french kiss was going on.* Yes, I was going to be inside the mouth—directing those tongues, instructing them in how to move, how to touch, how to swirl around one another. My muse had inspired me. It wasn't Cathy's mouth I was thinking about—although she did have a cute sardonic little smile. I was thinking about the Ideal Girl, an intellectual abstraction: the philosophical essence of the good, the beautiful, and the desirable. "I'm going to do what no man has ever done for the girl he loves," I said, speaking half aloud to myself. "What no man *could* ever do for the girl he loves. No one except me can do it because only I am the author of a best-selling book about kissing, and in the history of the world, no man—not Genghis Khan, not Napoleon, not Kennedy, not Khrushchev, not Einstein, not even D. H. Lawrence, *my hero*!, not one of these übermensch—had the audacity, the vision, or the barebones idea to project himself—his entire body—into the mouth of the Ideal Girl. Not one man in the whole history of the world had the opportunity or the idea to do it. Only me!" And I was going to make the most of it.

I set about my plan with a vengeance. It pleased me to think that even though my audience couldn't see me at the moment, they must be connected to me through some kind of extrasensory perception, through some numinous ethereal link. Millions of people would sense what I was doing without my even having to tell them. Of course I would show them eventually, and they would see it on the DVD, but even *before* that they would feel it magnetically. Crazy thoughts like this were spurring me on with my preproduction work.

I hired a young man; thin, intelligent, handsome. He was a props man. His job was to build the tongues.

It occurred to me that once he built the tongues he might have some spiritual connection with my future audience himself, simply by virtue of having constructed these all-important props. But as it turned out, he had no such designs on my audience; instead, he was perfectly willing to work in the background and let me reap all the glory. He called me one day and said, "Can I bring a boy to the set?"

"A boy?"

"A young man."

"Sure, why not?"

"He's going to be my assistant."

"I see."

"He's going to help construct the tongues."

"Very good then."

"Do you want them to be dripping?"

"What?"

"I mean so that they're wet."

"Why would I want that?"

"To look like real tongues. The saliva. I could make them out of rubber and drizzle honey or syrup over them to look realistic—"

"No, no, no."

"You're sure?"

"Keep them dry. I don't want to get wet or sticky when I'm in the mouth with them."

"You're going *into* the mouth with them?"

"Yes, of course."

"So they should be soft, right?"

"Yes, soft like real tongues. And flexible."

"I'm on it!"

When I got off the phone I smiled to myself. My props man sounded like one of the most creative people in my crew. But I was a little worried about his honey suggestion, which struck me as overkill. Thankfully, I had had that opportunity to talk with him and describe what I wanted.

The day for the tongue scene arrived, bright and sunny. It was the last day of the shoot. The props man brought me two hollow eight-foot rubber tubes, painted red, with little rubber bumps on them. The only problem was that they didn't look like tongues. More than anything else they looked like two oversize phalluses.

"How do they look?"

"Fine."

"Are you sure they're okay?"

"Absolutely."

I had no choice. Because it was the last day of the shoot, I had no more reservations with the camera operator. I had no time for any revisions to be made with the tongues. I was compelled to use them as they were.

I suspended a red sheet between two grip stands, arranged a spotlight behind the sheet to project light onto it, and in front of this I had two actors insert their heads and hands into the rubber tongues. The whole thing looked hellish, with the red light shining through the sheet and these two huge rubber tongues getting ready to do a french kiss for the camera. Then I slipped into the middle of the setup, and the camera started rolling. I was wearing thick-framed plastic glasses, and I began to speak.

"Hi, friends. Here I am inside a huge mouth to show you how to move your tongue for a french kiss."

The tongues got closer, and I pulled them together. One of them hit me in the face and knocked my glasses off.

"The first thing you want to do is touch the tips of your tongues. The tip of the tongue is the most sensitive part of the body. It has more nerve endings per square inch than anyplace else. And it can taste things too. It can taste the sweetness of your partner's tongue. Go ahead— flicker your tongues!"

The two tongues moved blindly up and down, missing each other by a foot. I guided them closer so that the tips finally touched, and I slowed the action down.

"This feels heavenly. Do you see how exciting it is to touch the tip of your partner's tongue?"

All I was thinking about was how ridiculous it was going to look and how my muse was going to laugh herself silly when she saw it.

The other thing I was hoping was that she would never again be able to do a french kiss with any man—boyfriend, lover, or husband—without picturing yours truly inside her mouth, guiding her tongue. That was the mental virus I wished to plant in her brain. I would always be there for her most intimate kisses. She'd never again be able to kiss any guy without me being part of that kiss. That was precisely what I wanted! Because if I could plant an idea like that in *one girl's* mind, it's proof positive that I could transmit the same idea to millions of other viewers. This is why you have a muse in the first place. If you can move *her*, you can move the world.

We shot the DVD in two weeks with a cast and crew of more than thirty people and a production budget of $6,000. One of the highlights of the project was my appearance inside that giant mouth. Viewers found it hilarious. We also included some comic scenes in a Boston hospital about a girl who required medical attention after becoming starved for oxygen during a french kiss—something, friends, that never actually happens. The DVD was so popular that people kept violating my copyright and uploading copies to YouTube. Eventually I gave up fighting them and came to regard their intellectual property rights infringement the way the Chinese do, considering it a compliment that they admired my work.

But this was merely the first small step on a journey that would take me to the edge of exhaustion as my lecture agents booked me on literally hundreds of college and university stages, and even on national television, going into one humongous mouth after another with those oversize tongues, doing the same routine again and again before millions of people.

And how did my muse react to it when she finally returned from Las Vegas and saw me inside that huge mouth? As expected, like everyone else she enjoyed seeing me make a fool of myself.

CHAPTER TWENTY-SIX

THE MUTE INTERVIEW

"HELLO, IS THIS WILLIAM CANE?"

"Hunh?

"William, is that you?"

"Uh . . . It's two in the morning—"

"Oh, I'm terribly sor—"

"Who's calling?"

"I'm so sorry. This is Lucy, a producer for BBC Liverpool. I must have gotten the time zone wrong."

Someone with an English accent had rung my phone at two in the morning, jarring me out of a deep sleep. As my mind refocused on her voice, she was saying, "We'd love for you to come to Liverpool and be interviewed on national television about your kissing book."

Then she told me that the British television station would cover all my expenses. Suddenly the prospect of a free visit to England loomed before my sleep-numbed brain. I quickly checked my calendar and verified that I would not be teaching during the three days required for the trip. Before I got off the phone I had agreed to travel to Liverpool. Try going back to sleep after a call like that! Not an easy task, to say the least. I thought I would have a wonderful time in England, receive some free international publicity, and be the envy of all my friends and family. I never guessed that I was setting myself up for one of the most embarrassing experiences of my life.

In those days I was a deep sleeper, all right. When I got on that plane to London at five in the evening, making a connection to Liverpool, I was excited and thought I'd do a terrific job in my interview with the BBC, but by the time I checked in to my hotel in Liverpool, washed my face, and changed my clothes for the interview it was midnight New York time, and by the time the limo picked me up to take me to the studio it was one thirty in the morning and I was getting tired. Even being in the green room and surrounded by all the hoopla that precedes a live television appearance didn't help, because by the time I got through makeup and hair and all the rehearsals and pep talks with the producers and was ushered into the studio for the interview, it was three thirty in the morning by my clock.

"And here's our guest from New York, William Cane, author of the international bestseller *The Art of Kissing.*"

I could barely keep my eyes open.

The host was a stocky fellow in a blue suit, sitting next to his cohost, a tall blonde in a red blouse and white slacks. They were smiling at me. We were on live television. In England it was nine thirty in the morning, but I was almost asleep.

"What was the most surprising thing you discovered when doing your research?"

I knew I had been asked something and I tried to answer them. But for the life of me, I couldn't open my mouth. My brain had gone to sleep.

The two hosts looked at me in some consternation.

"That was a question, William."

"Um . . ."

I know I made a complete fool of myself on live national British television, but the people in the production office were very kind about it. They had wasted all this money to fly me over, buy me a hotel room, pay for my meals, and I had been a mute—a deaf and dumb mute. I could not say a word. I felt terribly ashamed. But there was nothing I could do to bring my mind to a state of wakefulness in that studio. In those days, like I said, I was a deep sleeper, and at three in the morning, no matter what was going on in the world around me, I was asleep. Put me in a television studio if you want, but I'm still going to be slumbering on my feet.

When I returned to the green room a production assistant came up to me. I thought she was going to chew me out, but she said, "A reporter wants to interview you for a magazine story if you have time."

"When?"

"In three hours, at twelve thirty this afternoon."

"All right," I said. "That's six thirty in the morning New York time. I'll be awake by then. Is there someplace I can close my eyes for a while?"

She laughed and left the room. She didn't think I was serious. I guess she had missed my botched interview. I tried to close my eyes, but in a television production office with all those lights there are never any dark places where you can snooze, and for international travelers this can be nearly psychosis-inducing.

I must have dozed off for a few minutes, but everything between that moment and the time I stepped into the cafeteria downstairs for my interview with the reporter is wiped clean from my memory. But when I saw who was sitting at the table waiting to interview me, everything came into clear focus and I woke up.

The journalist sitting at the table was about twenty-four, and the first thing I noticed about her was that her eyes had the most friendly expression. I wondered how I'd ever get through the interview and then fly home to the United States with two crushing defeats: a mute television interview and then another humiliating interview with a young woman who could never really be interested in my work.

To my utter amazement, when I sat down she smiled warmly and I had to pinch myself to see if I was dreaming.

"Hello, I'm Nancy Lake," she said. "I'm a freelance reporter and I'm doing an article for a national magazine." I forget the name of her magazine; I could hardly concentrate because the magnetism of this young woman was so overpowering.

But the amazing thing was that she wasn't acting as if this were simply a routine interview with some crackpot author, as some American reporters had; instead, she appeared genuinely curious, asked several questions that she had written on her yellow pad of paper, and took copious notes on what I said. Then she went off her notes and improvised questions, demonstrating a real interest in the subject, which further amazed me. What a pleasant bit of culture shock! In my experience, there's a noticeable difference between Europeans and people Stateside. I've been to almost every state in the union, and the people I encountered were rarely as relaxed, personable, and friendly as those I met in England. Although Nancy didn't have to ask any more questions, she continued to chat with me about my work and her writing career. I even got a chance to ask about her birth order: she was a last born with one older sister. I like knowing the family constellation of interviewers because it helps me understand something about their temperament. In 2008 I would publish a book about birth order and how it affects personality, and I would even do presentations about it on the college lecture circuit. This reporter had all the open-mindedness and affability that research associates with younger sisters. Add to that her European demeanor, and we were really almost destined to have a good conversation.

At one point she asked me about the electric kiss, which I devote an entire chapter to in my book.

"You can receive a static electric shock by taking off a wool sweater in the winter," I said. "Or rolling around on a shaggy rug."

She laughed and blushed.

"Oh, I can't print *that*."

"Why not?"

"Because of the word you used."

"What word?"

She giggled and looked embarrassed, but I had no clue what she was talking about.

"I don't understand—"

"Oh, I don't know if I can explain it then," she said. "It's a difference between American and British English, and the word you used is a term that means something else."

"Do you mind telling me which word?"

"Um . . . ...shaggy."

"Wow, I never knew that. I'll have to remember not to use it if I go back on television."

"By the way, how did your interview go?"

When I told her that I had made a fool of myself on national television, she laughed and told me not to worry about it. And then she invited me back to her apartment.

Yes, this total stranger invited me to visit her apartment. I thought I must be dreaming again, but I was awake and it was real, and before I knew what was happening we were walking through the quaint streets of Liverpool together. She mentioned that she was proud to live in the city where the Beatles had gotten their start. I asked about bookstores—which I always like to visit when I'm in a new location—and she told me that there was a Waterstones within walking distance of my hotel. Fifteen minutes later we went up three flights of stairs, and she produced a key and opened the door to her living room. I expected she'd be living with her boyfriend, but it was a small one-bedroom flat, and it looked like she lived there alone.

"Would you like a soda?" she said, opening her refrigerator.

I was too nervous to eat or drink.

"No, thank you."

On the wall next to the refrigerator stood a life-size cutout of a Playboy bunny. When Nancy saw me looking at it she smiled.

"I used to be a Playboy bunny in the London club."

"Really?"

"Yes, but I stopped. I'm a reporter now and I'm putting all my energies into my writing career."

In the United States it would be unthinkable for a female reporter to invite a guy up to her apartment after just meeting him for a ten-minute interview. This brought home to me the striking difference between our two cultures.

After chatting with her for a few minutes and inquiring about her career plans and education, I realized that I had to get back to my hotel to prepare for my trip home. I tend to think that international visitors are somehow more attractive to women for some reason. D. H. Lawrence propounded a theory about the way that women become drawn to strangers. Yes, strange men might be dangerous, but on the flip side they can also be stimulating and novel in a way that a fellow countryman might not be, and that's the only reason I can think of why this captivating young woman asked me for a kiss before I left.

Now, of course I entertained the idea of pushing my luck and giving her an intimate kiss, especially after talking for an hour about kissing and making out . . . but it struck me as the wrong thing to do with a young woman who had been so generous with her time and hospitality. Instead, I gave her a chaste little kiss on the lips, adding a touch of the sliding kiss for good measure.

My heart glowed with a vague wistful feeling as I strolled back to my hotel. All the stupidity and embarrassment of being mute on national British television had been completely wiped away by that friendly kiss, and a white flash seemed to recurrently detonate inside my brain over the next few hours, eradicating all my mistakes and misgivings on this trip so that I felt like a brand-new man.

But when I got home and reported these shenanigans to my lecture agents, they threatened to add a contract clause prohibiting me from making out with anyone while traveling.

CHAPTER TWENTY-SEVEN

THE NECK KISS

I LIKE TO BE COMPLETELY UP FRONT WITH readers of my books, so I'm going to reveal how I got the idea for the neck-kiss scenario, something that was so electrifying for audiences that many people have asked about its origin.

I need to go back in time to when I was at the impressionable age of twenty-eight to begin this story. It was a balmy summer day, and I had taken a shortcut across the Boston University campus while heading home from an afternoon run along the Charles River. I had no inkling that I was headed into strange and dangerous waters.

An open door in the law school auditorium caught my eye, and I thought I'd peek in and see what was going on, maybe even catch a free movie. It was pitch-black inside, and it wasn't a movie but a lecture. The room was filled to capacity, and I stood in the back with a bunch of students and watched a ruggedly good-looking man gesture with a laser pointer at a huge image of an ice cube on the screen. It was so quiet you could hear a pin drop . . . until the students in the auditorium recognized what the speaker was outlining in that ice cube—and then a collective gasp rose from the crowd.

Now everyone could clearly see that the letters *S-E-X* had been hidden—*embedded* is the technical term—in the craggy surface of the ice. Slide after slide mesmerized the audience—and me—and sparked my lifelong interest in subliminal advertising. The speaker's name was Wilson Bryan Key.

When I worked at the Boston Arts Group later that year, Lauren Harper, the theater's publicist, taught me more about subliminal advertising. Lauren had short black hair and was in her late twenties. She acted like your aunt—a flirtatious aunt—and she always had guys buzzing about her like flies. "I studied it at Harvard Business School," she said, arching one eyebrow. "Most people don't believe it works, which is good for *us* since we can embed things in our posters that will draw more audience members to our productions, and they don't even know what's attracting them." She smiled mysteriously and handed me one of the posters she had designed. I didn't see anything significant at first . . . until she pointed to a long dirigible that she had added to the background. It was a shape any Freudian would have interpreted easily as a floating phallus, and it had been hidden in plain sight in the poster.

A few months later I enrolled as an undergrad at Boston College, where I majored in political science. I was older than most of my classmates because I had taken a seven-year leave of absence from Fordham. At Boston College I joined the Fulton Debating Society and was elected president of the club. In 1981 we debated Harvard on the issue of subliminal advertising. Our team took the position that subliminal advertising is highly effective, while Harvard had the task of trying to convince the audience that it didn't work. We won the debate in part because we mentioned that the Harvard team couldn't really argue that subliminal advertising didn't work, could they, when their own business school offered courses teaching publicists how to use it! Shortly after this I became friends with Wilson Bryan Key, who was a star on the college lecture circuit. In 1981 he published his third book about subliminal advertising, *The Clam-Plate Orgy and Other Subliminal Techniques for Manipulating Your Behavior*. The cover depicted a Howard Johnson's place mat featuring a dish of fried clams. In the book he convincingly demonstrates how the fried clams have been airbrushed and arranged to depict donkeys and humans engaging in sexual acts together, a veritable orgy on a place mat. This sneaky advertisement was clearly intended to prompt people to buy more food. The way it works is that sexual images on the place mat stimulate purchases, even of items people wouldn't ordinarily eat. These subliminal messages are all the more effective because people don't believe they're present and they don't see them consciously, but the unconscious is ultrasensitive to these stimuli, and research by psychologists and physiologists, including N. F. Dixon and others, demonstrates that below-threshold stimuli reach the brain and also affect human behavior.

Undoubtedly that place mat was still on my mind in 1999 while I was directing a series of nineteen interstitials for MTV. These promotional videos featured local actors dancing, talking, and doing various other visually arresting things for a few seconds, after which the network logo appeared. I had rented an apartment on

Commonwealth Avenue for two weeks to film this project. The rental agent's office was located on the first floor, and when she saw lights, cameras, and technicians pouring into the building, together with numerous young girls, some only eleven and twelve, she called the police. Right in the middle of our shoot there was a loud knock on the door, and I opened it to find two Boston cops demanding entry. We had a twelve-year-old girl in her pajamas in bed in the next room and I was reluctant to allow the police to see that because of all the explaining that I would have to do. "Have you officers got a warrant to enter?"

They replied, "We're here to see if any minors are in danger."

I stepped aside and let them in. At the time, there were about fifty cast and crew members in this one-bedroom apartment, including actors in costume and mothers and fathers of the minor children. My actors and their parents watched in annoyance as the police conducted their search. The first thing the officers discovered was a bulletin board in the living room with my storyboards for the day's shooting tacked up on it, one of which was captioned *The Orgy*. I knew from reading Wilson Key's work that many people were curious about orgies but that they repressed their interest and didn't acknowledge it consciously. So one of the MTV clips would involve two young women kissing a young man on the couch. I called it an orgy scene, but the actors would be fully clothed and the caption describing the skit was only used ironically. Unfortunately, when the police saw the storyboard they mistakenly thought that we had planned to film an actual orgy, and with this incorrect idea in their mind, they entered the bedroom and found the twelve-year-old girl under the covers. They were about to arrest me when I pointed out that the girl also had an MTV logo on her upper arm, and I asked the director of photography to replay the film that we had just shot of her simply rolling over in bed to reveal the tattoo. In other words, there was no orgy. Even more convincing was the fact that the girl's mother was sitting in the living room, and she assured the officers that no hanky-panky had been involved. And that's how I narrowly avoided being arrested.

Then fate stepped into the picture once more, in a very personal and surprising way. It happened when Wilson Key was eighty-two years old. He called me in February, and he sounded excited.

"I'm in a movie!" he said.

"Are you serious?"

"Do you know what it's about?"

"No, what?"

"Subliminal images in religious art."

"I'd love to see it."

"It's coming to New York."

I started laughing. I knew that he had devoted his life to exposing subliminal messages, and to think that he had been featured in a movie in his eighties pleased me tremendously. I was proud and happy for him. I went to see the film, entitled *Rape of the Soul*, and it depicted many of the same themes he explored in his books. Seeing him discussing his work on the screen of a Manhattan theater made me realize that many other people had a similar interest. In fact, Homo sapiens are more adept at different sexual practices than almost any other animals, except perhaps the bonobos, a species of sexually adventurous primates. Whereas most animals engage in sex only for reproduction, humans and bonobos enjoy sex for the purpose of bonding and for sheer hedonistic pleasure; both species even practice homosexuality and orgies. One suggestive piece of evidence proving that humans engage in sex for socialization is our creation of contraceptives, which no other animal uses, and which allows humans to enjoy sex for the sake of sex without leading to reproduction. So I started to think that maybe I should incorporate some of these orgy themes into the kissing show.

This line of reasoning, of course, led to my choreographing the group kiss, with the demonstrators crawling around onstage as if they were blind during a power failure, after which they would start groping each other and then eventually spill off the stage and move into the audience. The way the Cornell crowd had reacted with explosive laughter to the mention of the orgy in Risley Hall was the final piece of the puzzle that led me to one of my most popular innovations, and one that I'm proud to have dreamed up for the show. But like I've mentioned previously, it was really fate ordaining the interest I developed in orgies: from that first slide show I saw Bill Key deliver at Boston University, right down through all the other incidents that impressed upon me how interested human beings naturally are in group sexual practices.

I decided that what we needed was not a real orgy, or even a make-believe orgy, but merely the *suggestion* of one during the neck kiss.

The neck kiss involves boys kissing the necks of their partners. My survey of more than a hundred thousand people in twenty-three countries and all across the United States revealed that of all the places women like to be kissed their favorite spot, aside from the mouth, happens to be the neck. The survey also revealed that girls are ten times more excited by neck kisses than guys. So whenever we demonstrated the neck kiss, we had the *guys* kiss the *girls*: this was the most realistic way to show it. The skit involved all the girls standing facing the audience while the boys kissed their necks, and then the boys moved behind the girls and kissed them on the back of the neck. In many cases, both during rehearsal and during the show, girls who received neck kisses would laugh, giggle, moan in pleasure, and get weak in the knees and have to be supported by their partners; sometimes they would even collapse into their chairs or onto the floor. This kind of reaction caused audiences to scream with delight.

But my next development took a good thing and made it even better. I instructed the girls to sit in their chairs after they had been kissed on the neck, and I asked the boys to step aside and pretend that they were away at school or work.

"Girls enjoy neck kisses so much," I told the audience. "But we guys forget, and it's because neck kisses may thrill our girlfriends but these kinds of kisses don't do much for us. And here's where we make our big mistake: the girl is sitting at home waiting for her husband or boyfriend to return from work or school, and *what* do we do? Instead of going home and giving her a *neck* kiss, we return to her—"

The boys put one knee on their chairs and leaned toward the girls as I continued narrating—

"—and we give her a boring . . . *cheek* kiss."

The boys kissed the girls' cheeks.

"—and she's thinking, if only . . . *If only* . . . If only

Joe was here . . . because Joe used to kiss my neck . . . And then magically . . . Joe *is* there—"

The boys had been carefully choreographed by me in rehearsal to move to the next chair and kiss this new girl's neck. The boy on the house-right end of the line ran around to the first girl and kissed her neck, while all the other guys moved to the next girl in line. The first time we did this skit the audience began to scream. But I didn't stop there; I continued my story—

"—and Joe kisses her *neck*. He kisses up and down her neck, under her chin, in back of her neck. He kisses her like she's never been kissed before . . . *Next house, guys!*"

Again the boys switched partners and moved to the next girl, and the audience roared with laughter. We continued in this fashion until we'd made the switch three or four times. The audience reaction built to a crescendo, right up to the conclusion of the skit, when I closed it by saying:

"You hear a car in the driveway! Go home! You remember where home was, don't you? Your original girl."

The boys quickly returned to their original partners, and I continued directing:

"Dry her off—"

They wiped their partner's neck.

"—and . . . kiss her *neck*."

I finished the skit by turning to the audience and smiling.

"Men, I'm only telling you this to save you emotional problems . . . because if *you* don't kiss her neck—Joe will!"

The neck kiss, with its suggestive partner switching, quickly became one of the high points of the show. Then after I had been using it successfully for a few months, a funny thing happened during a performance in Tennessee. Unknown to me, we had a brother and sister onstage in different couples. During the neck kiss, when the boys had to kiss the other girls, this young man came to his sister and froze.

"What are you waiting for?" I demanded.

The audience started laughing. At this cozy little college everybody knew everybody else, and they knew it was his sister.

"Kiss that girl!" I said.

The boy's face turned red and finally, at my urging, he leaned down and kissed his sister.

The audience rewarded this ridiculous development with side-splitting peals of laughter. After the show, one of his friends told me the truth about them being brother and sister, and I went up to the boy and apologized. "I'm sorry!" I said. "I would never have asked you to kiss her if I had known."

He laughed, and I saw that both he and his sister were ultimately all right with the way the scene had gone. They realized that I hadn't known their relationship. I never wanted to embarrass my demonstrators, so I took this mistake as a lesson. In the future I tried to get a sense of the relationship of the volunteers in the demonstrator couples, but luckily I never had to deal with this same situation again.

I've often asked myself why the neck kiss turned out to be one of the most exciting skits in the kissing show. I believe it was because fate had sent me in a direction that most people never pursue: I experienced that formative exposure to the work of Wilson Bryan Key on subliminal advertising, and I began to appreciate that people are often tickled by unconscious sexual impulses and images. In addition, I had studied Key's work on the many ways that advertisers hide orgies in advertisements in order to stir up subliminal interest and increase sales. Then I saw how the police had seized upon my innocent storyboard simply because it was captioned *The Orgy*. Last but not least, I had been impressed by the way that my friend had participated in a movie about hidden sexual content. All these experiences made me feel pretty sure that college audiences would respond to the merest suggestion of an orgy in a skit. Having the boys switch couples and kiss all the girls onstage was enough to push the audience's imagination into overdrive. Still, I can't take full credit for coming up with the idea since I believe it was that old witch fate who tangled me up in her web and sent me down the perilous path to the neck kiss.

But old mother fate had one final cruel card to play, and when she dealt the next hand to me it nearly spelled the end of the kissing show—and of my life.

CHAPTER TWENTY-EIGHT

HOW I ALMOST DIED TWICE

MY PROBLEM IS I'M A PEOPLE PLEASER. LIKE many firstborn children I want people to like me, and if they raise objections I try to calm their nerves by doing what they want instead of thinking for myself. This tendency to please people got me in trouble with that final card fate dealt out of her deck of tricks.

"Billy, they want you up in Idaho."

I was on the phone with Kevin.

"I'd love to do a show there."

"But we have a problem—"

"What is it?"

"The only flight available is a small plane."

"That doesn't bother me."

"Are you sure?"

"If that's the only way to get there, then book my flight because I want to go."

"One of our other speakers refused to travel on this airline when he saw their planes."

"But I'm not like that. I used to be nervous about flying years ago. In fact, right after my book was published the producers at *Oprah* wanted to fly me out to Chicago. I asked whether I could travel by train. They never called back. So I learned my lesson, and I forced myself to overcome my fear of flying by taking flight after flight. Now I'm fearless."

"Okay, then I'll book the gig."

"I'm looking forward to it."

I got off the phone with Kevin and felt proud of myself, but three weeks later when I arrived at my connection in Boise, Idaho, I had a surprise waiting for me. There was nobody at the departure gate except one lanky guy standing beside the check-in desk. He was doing his best to hide the fact that he was smoking a cigarette. I walked over and struck up a conversation.

"It's quiet here today," I said.

"Are you going to Pocatello?"

"Yes. Are you headed there too?"

He stubbed out his cigarette and smiled.

"I'm your pilot."

A few minutes later he led me out onto the windy airfield himself. There were no other passengers in sight. On the tarmac sat the smallest airplane I had ever seen: it was, in fact, a two-seater. I couldn't believe what I had gotten myself into with this gig! I was also incredulous when the pilot told me I had to sit in the cockpit where the copilot normally sits. But he was perfectly serious. After I buckled myself into the seat beside the pilot, he nodded toward the floor in front of me and said, quite pointedly, "Whatever you do, keep your feet off that rudder pedal."

At these words, I cringed and drew my legs back as far as possible. I couldn't even see the pedal in the obscurity, but I knew it was there, and I knew instinctively that my life depended upon my following the pilot's instruction to the letter.

Our takeoff gave me a clear indication that this would not be a normal trip. Every vibration from the wheels jarred the base of my spine. I glanced over at the pilot: his jaw was set and his eyes behind blue goggles jumped rapidly back and forth over his flight panel.

I tried to maintain an open mind and enjoy the experience, but we climbed no higher than about a thousand feet and I could discern people walking in the fields below. Ten minutes into the flight a yellow bulb started blinking on the control panel. The pilot muttered something under his breath. Directly ahead, a vast multitude of dots rose into the sky.

"What's that?" I said.

"Mallard ducks."

The pilot gripped the tiller so hard his knuckles turned white.

"We'll go under them," he said grimly.

Suddenly our plane took a nose dive, and the pit of my stomach dropped out. We emerged from the descent through a swirl of feathers at treetop level. Some of the ducks had apparently strayed ahead of the flock. The sound of indignant quacking receded behind us.

I thought I had handled the experience pretty well, but when we landed at the airfield in Pocatello and I climbed out of the cockpit, my knees wobbled under me and I almost fainted from nervous exhaustion. I would have to do the show with the sure knowledge that I'd never get home unless I took a similar return flight back to Boise. I tried not to think about it, but the more I attempted to push it out of my mind, the more I realized that I had risked my life for the kissing show.

For the return trip I bought a million-dollar insurance

policy on my life. It was funny, however, when the flight to Boise turned out to be a seven-seater with four other passengers. Most of them looked white-faced with anxiety, but I sat there enjoying the feeling of security that this, to me, hugely luxurious aircraft provided. After that experience I never worried about small planes again.

But the next time I narrowly escaped death on the college lecture circuit was even worse.

Kevin and Jayne liked to save money on travel, and to accomplish this goal they often booked me on inexpensive airlines and selected connecting flights with layovers. This strategy resulted in my spending hours waiting in crowded airports all across the United States. And since takeoffs and landings are the most dangerous parts of air travel, the more connections I had to make, the more risky the trip. Still, I took comfort in the fact that statistics were overwhelmingly on my side, and I didn't worry too much about connecting flights. Then one day Kevin called, and he sounded very enthused.

"We can save $1,000 if you take the connecting flight from Harrisburg to Washington, DC, next week. Do you want to do it?"

"Sure, why not!"

"Great, I'll send you the itinerary."

I thought nothing of it because saving money on expenses was one of the things Kevin and Jayne did so well. But five minutes after we took off from Harrisburg, the pilot made a steep right turn. I had a window seat, and it was a clear, sunny afternoon. As we banked sharply, three monstrous funnels loomed ahead, each belching gray smoke into the sky. Our flight path looked like it would be taking us directly into the plume of that smoke.

The scene below us looked vaguely familiar too. I found myself troubled by an elusive memory, but I couldn't put my finger on exactly what was bothering me. A few seconds later my anxiety was confirmed when the captain made a startling announcement:

"We're passing over Three Mile Island, folks. If you look out your windows you'll have a good view of probably the most famous nuclear generating station in the United States."

People were craning their necks to see. The guy sitting to my right took one look and murmured under his breath, "Looks like we're headed directly into radioactive steam."

Unfortunately for me, his words proved eerily prophetic, and the sky gradually clouded as smoke obscured the windows.

"It's nuclear radiation!" a youngster behind me cried.

I held my breath, my heart hammering in my chest, counting the seconds we were engulfed: one thousand one . . . one thousand two . . . one thousand three . . . one thousand four . . . one thousand five . . . one thousand six . . . one thousand seven . . . Until finally we started coming out of it. I was cursing in my mind: Why had I let Kevin talk me into taking this economy flight directly over a nuclear power plant? This wasn't any old nuclear generating station either—this was the scene of one of the worst nuclear accidents in history. Even if our jet had a self-contained air system, how could you be sure that dangerous particles of radioactive material weren't penetrating into your lungs and circulating throughout your body? Nobody was addressing that question, and the captain never mentioned anything about the safety—or potential lethal danger—of flying through that reactor steam.

When I arrived on the campus of Georgetown University, where I was scheduled to do an eight o'clock show, I was a complete nervous wreck. I hadn't been able to rehearse in my hotel because my mind kept going over the way I had passed through that radiation.

"What's the matter?" the boy in charge of the event asked.

"I've been exposed to a dose of radioactive material," I said. "My plane flew over Three Mile Island, and everyone on board was complaining about it."

"Come with me," he said.

He pointed down an empty hall.

"Where are we going?"

"You'll see."

Presently we stopped beside a wooden door on which was posted a sign that announced:

CAUTION
RADIOACTIVE
MATERIAL

I had no desire to stand outside a laboratory containing additional radioactive material, especially when I had just been exposed to a potentially lethal dose from Three Mile Island. But the head of the entertainment committee said:

"I called Seth, a grad student."

"What good will that do me?"

"He'll be here in a minute."

I was getting more nervous with each passing second, but shortly thereafter a young man wearing glasses came up to us.

"Is this him?" he asked.

"Yes," the entertainment student said.

Seth unlocked the door and entered the laboratory. A minute later he emerged with a yellow box connected to a black cable that terminated in a cylindrical probe.

"Stand aside," Seth said, addressing me.

"What's that thing?"

"A Geiger counter."

He flicked a switch and a familiar—and highly startling—series of sounds emanated from the machine: *Click click click . . . click click . . . click click click!*

I almost jumped out of my skin, I was so devastated by the sound.

"How radioactive am I?"

"Wait a minute."

He fiddled with the dials.

"I'm adjusting it."

I felt ashamed to realize that I was holding my breath again, but after what seemed like an eternity those horrible clicks slowed and then stopped. Seth announced, "You're clear."

"Clear?"

"You're not dangerously radioactive."

"Oh, thank god! . . . Are you sure?"

"We learned to use Geiger counters this semester, and I'm pretty certain you're okay."

I heaved a sigh of relief. But as we walked toward the venue for my sound check, I started worrying again; after all, Seth was only a graduate student . . . what if he wasn't a competent operator of a Geiger counter? Shouldn't I seek the advice of a professional for a radiation test? I resolved to do that as soon as I returned home from my trip. When I finally made an appointment with a doctor in Boston and got a clean bill of health, I felt I could finally relax and put my Three Mile Island incident behind me. He claimed my fears had been groundless and that it wasn't possible to absorb deadly radiation while insulated by the fuselage of a commercial jet. But I swore to myself that never again would I allow my lecture agents to book me on an economy flight from Harrisburg to Washington, DC.

No, I would gladly pay extra to avoid risking my life again for the kissing show.

CHAPTER TWENTY-NINE

"DO THIS SHOW OR WE'RE THROUGH!"

SHOULD ANYONE DOUBT THAT KISSING appeals more to girls than guys, try this little test. Survey some young people and see who reacts more enthusiastically to the idea of kissing. After questioning more than a hundred thousand people, it became crystal clear to me that while guys do like to kiss, girls are hands down more interested than their boyfriends in the connection and intimacy involved in kissing. That's why they flocked to the kissing show.

I've directed more than three thousand college students in kissing demonstrations, and I've entertained more than a hundred thousand in live audiences at these shows, and the gender difference is clear. We usually drew an overwhelming preponderance of girls to the show. And most times the volunteers were girls who had dragged their reluctant boyfriends into the embarrassing experience of going onstage and kissing in front of hundreds of other people.

Because of this intense interest on the part of girls, and also because I wanted them to feel comfortable about doing the show, I often directed things in a way that would appeal to the female imagination. A high school friend of mine, Perry Lonardo, attended one of my performances in Indiana, and his response confirms that I achieved what I set out to do. There were 350 in attendance on the night he saw the show, and afterward we went to a local bar for drinks and he gave me some perceptive feedback.

"You've reinvented yourself," he said. "It was an amazing performance, and what struck me was how much it looked like a fashion show. The volunteers, what do you call them—?"

"Demonstrators."

"The demonstrators stand there kissing or saying nothing sometimes, as if frozen in tableaux, while music is playing in the background and you have spotlights raking across the stage. It's a spectacle."

This notion that the performance had some elements of a fashion show struck me as perfectly apt. I hadn't thought about that before, but as a general rule fashion shows do appeal more to girls than guys, and so did the kissing show. As I've mentioned, the audience was usually two-thirds girls, which is why I oriented the show toward them. This is also how I wrote the book, anticipating that my audience would be primarily female.

Shortly after *The Art of Kissing* was published I happened to be browsing in the Brookline Booksmith, and two girls who must have been no more than ten or eleven were sitting in the aisle on the floor paging through a copy of my book. They were giggling in enjoyment at what they were reading. I should have introduced myself to them, but I somewhat selfishly wanted to preserve that magical moment in my memory without any interference, so I said nothing. But the incident underscores how positively females responded to the book. You wouldn't find two guys sitting on a bookstore floor reading it in a million years.

I received an email recently from a fifteen-year-old girl who said, in an almost stunned, accusatory tone, "I absolutely could *not* put your book down and especially loved the chapter on the music kiss. But how is it that *you* know what girls like?" That, to me, was the nicest compliment I ever received, and a very gratifying remark to hear. Yes, I had aimed the book at girls, had tried to figure out what they would like, and had surveyed them to find out their innermost thoughts. Apparently, I had succeeded. My literary agent, Marla Glading, my initial editor, Barbara Anderson, and my subsequent editor after Barbara departed from St. Martin's Press, Marian Lizzi, all left their sensibilities on the book too, helping it become successful with girls all over the world.

There's no better proof of the way that girls were the focus of this show than some of the funny things that happened during various performances. At Lafayette College in Easton, Pennsylvania, a cute blonde and her handsome boyfriend volunteered to be one of the couples. It was a Valentine's theme show on February 1, 2000, and the stage was decorated with red and white hearts. But I noticed during rehearsal that the boy didn't seem too enthusiastic about the whole thing; although he did all the demonstrations, he didn't have the eagerness that you like to see in a performer. But since I can't change the cast once I arrive at a school, I was forced to put him on with his girlfriend. During the show the same pattern of lackadaisical performance persisted. This wasn't the worst thing in the world, because I had three other couples and I could direct the audience's attention wherever I wished simply by pointing or telling the audience that couple number one, for instance, was doing something noteworthy. After the show was over, however, I learned the truth and the story behind this boy's reticence. One of the girls from the entertainment committee took me aside and told me what had happened.

"His girlfriend threatened him, saying, 'Either you do this show or we're through!'"

"Are you serious?"

"Yes, she really wanted to do it, but he didn't."

I smiled to myself. So, that explained it! The poor fellow had been dragged into it against his will. I was glad it wasn't *me* who had been in that position, because when your girlfriend asks you to do something it's hard to resist. Like a smart young man he had made the right choice. As Ovid observes with his customary levity in *The Art of Love*, we must please our partners in these small things in order to maintain peace.

I arrived at the last minute for a show in Baltimore due to travel delays, and as I was approaching the venue I suddenly found the campus path blocked by a sea of students. *What on earth put all these kids on this path and directly in my way?* It was frustrating and hard to get through the press of young people, especially with them surging forward and trying to squeeze through the same door. As I nudged by, I asked one of them, "Where are you going?" and he smiled and said something that tickled me.

"We're going to *The Art of Kissing*."

"Don't worry," I said. "You won't miss anything. I'm directing the show, and I just got here."

By the time I made my way into the building and apologized to the young man from the student activities office for the unexpected delay, there was no opportunity to rehearse. The venue was a five-hundred-capacity auditorium with steeply raked fixed seats, like those old-fashioned operating theaters where doctors perform experimental procedures for medical students. The place was jam-packed and every seat filled.

With no time for rehearsal, and only two couples waiting to be given instruction, I solicited additional volunteers from the audience. Miraculously, a third couple came down from their seats, and they happened to be stunningly good-looking. The girl was a tall blonde, and her boyfriend looked like James Dean. I took the three couples aside and told them that there was no time for rehearsal, and I asked them to do everything that I instructed them to do during the show, even if it seemed unusual. I assured them that I had directed the show many times and that if they would simply follow my instructions during the performance, they would be fine.

"And that includes the vacuum kiss, the group kiss, and the spanking kiss, where you spank your partner—"

"Oh no," the new boy said. "We can't do partner switching. And we can't do the spank."

Good grief, I thought, here are two attractive kids, and of course the eyes of all five hundred people in the audience are going to be on them every time they refuse to do a demonstration. This last couple was going to be the least capable of my demonstrators, the most shy, and the ones who were going to make this show fall apart. I knew right away that the boy was fearful of having any other guys kiss his girlfriend, and the girl went along with his restriction, or had the same fear herself. Of course, if she had voted otherwise, the same thing might have happened as at Lafayette College, where the girl had dragged her unwilling boyfriend into the show. In the final analysis, girls always controlled how the show progressed, and this particular girl was the determining factor. At any other school, I would have prohibited them from being in the show, preferring a couple that could do all the demonstrations and not make the performance look choppy by stopping midstream every time we got to a kiss that was too much for them to handle, but here I was up against the clock and I needed this third couple, so we went ahead, and whenever we came to a group kiss or a switch skit, like the neck kiss, these two kids stepped aside and put a damper on all the fun.

Girls were again the rulers of the day at a Maryland college where I arrived to find that the student in charge of the event had not been able to round up a single volunteer. With time running out, I quickly walked around the entire student union looking for demonstrators. I finally found one couple in the cafeteria. Then I succeeded in convincing an easygoing and handsome young man to volunteer, promising to get him a partner before showtime. He was very cooperative and I liked his attitude. I had a feeling that he was going to be fun to work with no matter who I found for his partner. With only thirty minutes left before the performance was scheduled to start, I happened to notice two girls walking down the hallway together. They were apparently close friends. I'd noticed over the course of many shows that when you find two girls who are friends and who are in a good mood— something I could clearly see because they were smiling and talking animatedly with one another—there is a certain dynamic at work where if you approach them in the right way, you can sometimes prompt them to take a risk together and jump into the public spotlight. The secret is to play them off one another, and this was exactly the strategy I planned to use. This time, at my side, helping me find girls, was the guy who was single and didn't have a partner. I figured that one of these girls would volunteer to be with him, and I approached them with that in mind.

"How would you girls like to be in a kissing show?" I said. I didn't have time to waste and had to get right to the point.

They stopped and listened politely.

"It's a kissing demonstration scheduled by your school's entertainment committee, and we need one more girl to kiss this guy."

The girls gave the guy the once-over. Naughty smiles appeared on their faces and they giggled. What could they be thinking? Then they turned the tables on me in an unexpected way. The brunette replied for both of them: "We'll do it if we can *both* kiss him."

I was stunned at the request. This had never happened at any other school, and I had to make sure I understood what they were demanding.

"You *both* want to kiss him?"

"Yes."

"But what if I can get you another guy—"

"No, no, then we *won't* do it."

I turned to the boy, and he smiled. Bless his soul, he had no objection. And why would he? Before him lay the alluring prospect of being kissed by two cute girls.

The way we set it up, the blonde would kiss the boy

during the first half of the show, and then at a prearranged signal her friend would take over as the boy's partner for the remainder of the performance. At the opening of the show, I explained this arrangement to the audience so that they wouldn't be puzzled when the switchover occurred. The first girl did a wonderful job during her half of the action, and the second did an equally good job during her half. Strangely enough, I got the impression that these girls liked sharing a partner, and in the back of my mind I was wondering whether their preference had anything to do with the subconscious idea of an orgy. After the show the boy thanked me warmly, and I saw the two girls exiting the room with those same wicked smiles on their faces. Yes, they had been the stars of that performance, and I felt fortunate to have had them participate.

One final story will illustrate the way that girls ruled the kissing show.

At the University of Virginia, the student in charge, Nathan, was a personable young man who had rounded up three couples to be demonstrators. These were kids who were dating, so they had no hesitation about kissing, but the stage was set with eight chairs and I hoped we could find a girl from the audience to pair up with the student executive. "Why don't you sit through the rehearsal, Nathan, and pretend there's a girl with you, okay? You just kiss the air and use your imagination, and that will prepare *you* for the performance. This way, if we find a girl at the last minute, at least *you'll* have been rehearsed."

Surprisingly, he was game, and he went along with this arrangement. He was a good-looking, square-chinned fellow with neatly combed brown hair, but I felt sorry for him because all throughout the rehearsal the three other couples were laughing at the way he stood at the end of the line with his hands up around an invisible girl. And, poor fellow, when he had to do the kisses in rehearsal, he would close his eyes and pucker up and execute those kisses on this imaginary girl. It was a somewhat pathetic sight, and I felt terrible by the end of rehearsal. I was sure he would go home unrequited and without a partner.

When we emerged from our private rehearsal room in the student activities office, we were greeted by a totally packed house—three hundred in the audience and not a chair empty. The preshow music was rocking the crowd and everyone was in a cheerful mood—the perfect college audience—so I had a good feeling about the performance to come, even though the poor fellow who had kissed an imaginary girl would have no partner. As my three couples took their seats onstage, I placed Nathan all the way house right next to an empty chair.

"Is there any girl who would like to volunteer to be with him?" I said. As an added incentive to get things moving, I added, "If you know a girl who should volunteer, point to her for me and send her up here." Suddenly several people pointed to one of their friends, pressuring her to come up on the stage and join the show. This was all the motivation that this particular girl needed, and she bounded energetically out of her seat and stepped up to the stage to take the empty seat next to Nathan. She was an attractive blonde, and she was clearly unafraid and enthusiastic; in fact, she completely surprised me by being extremely confident even though she didn't know what we had planned and she hadn't rehearsed.

I was relieved that Nathan finally had a partner, and I stepped behind the girl and whispered some words of encouragement: "Just listen to what I'm saying and glance at the other girls and you'll be fine." I was worried about her, but I tried not to let it show.

Very soon after the demonstrations started, though, it became clear that this girl was going to steal the show. She was so adept at doing the skits that she fascinated the audience. Her partner was a serious young fellow, and it was funny to see how the girl teased him by smiling coyly and running her fingers through his hair whenever she had the opportunity. In the middle of the show, the audience started giggling unexpectedly, and I heard a few girls whispering and gasping. I happened to be out in the audience at the time, and I covered the microphone and asked them what was going on. They didn't answer, but they pointed at Nathan, and I immediately saw what had caused all the laughter: he was standing with both hands crossed over the front of his pants, and his partner had a smile of self-satisfied triumph on her face.

After the show we took a vote on which couple was most entertaining, and not surprisingly Nathan and this uninhibited girl won hands down. They received a copy of *The Art of Kissing* DVD that I had produced. A few minutes later, while I was packing up my props, Nathan came up to me and said something I'll never forget:

"This was the best night of my college life."

CHAPTER THIRTY

COLORADO SCHOOL OF MINES

"YOU GOT AN OFFER FROM THE COLORADO School of Mines."

"Colorado School of—*what*?"

"Mines."

"What kind of school is that?"

"Engineering."

"Are you joking?"

"Do I ever joke about offers?"

That's how Kevin began the phone conversation, and it totally floored me.

"What would a school like Mines want with me?"

"They're kids," he said. "They need entertainment."

The reason I was floored by this offer is easily explained. Interest in the show had increased year by year, and I had been doing more gigs each semester. But for this trend to continue unabated I needed to speak at schools that had curricula far removed from my interests and far removed from the show's focus. I was being thrust onto stages before hundreds of college students at business and science schools that I feared I could never connect with or entertain. True enough, I liked making the money, and the pay was exceptional, especially now that the Contemporary Issues Agency had raised my asking price, but at the same time I didn't want to misrepresent myself and promise that I could hold the interest of an audience of engineers, for example, at a school like Mines.

But Kevin convinced me that I could do it, and that in reality the audience would be no different from the kids at any other college. Maybe they would be a trifle more focused on science and engineering, but they were still college kids and they would have the same high levels of hormones that I had encountered at every other college. My agent assured me that there was no way a kissing show could fail to please them.

Yes, Kevin put all that in my ear, and before I knew it I was on a plane winging my way to Golden, Colorado, on January 28, 2000. During the flight I started dozing as I usually do on long airplane trips, and while in a half-asleep state I began to have a vision: I imagined a long dark mine shaft that went down hundreds of feet and then leveled off. Crawling along that mine shaft came a girl, and on her head she wore a miner's cap with a bright light that illuminated a narrow cone of yellow in front of her. At the other end of the tunnel, a boy with a similar cap and light inched his way toward the girl, his beam of light illuminating the area in front of him. Suddenly I started forward in my seat and almost knocked myself out on the headrest in front of me. *What if . . . what if*, I was thinking, *what if—*

I wanted to shout, but I stifled my excitement.

—what if those two young miners happened to be lovers who were lost in a mine shaft, and what if right at the beginning of the show I arranged for two students to enact this romantic scenario in a darkened theater, playacting how they got separated and then reunited in an abandoned mine . . . and what's more, what if I could get the school to provide miner's hats with working lights, just like honest-to-goodness miners wear! I was ecstatic with this vision, and I kept replaying and fine-tuning it in my mind. Naturally, the skit wouldn't work at any other school, but at the Colorado School of Mines it had to work—it *had* to be a hit—it had to be a smash sensation. And this would be a perfect setup for the rest of the performance. The cute meeting in the mine would situate the kissing show perfectly in the realm of engineering, paving the way for the rest of the program to appeal to the scientific mind-set of this particular audience. At least that's how I imagined it would work, but as Schopenhauer is fond of telling us, in real life things don't always turn out the way you planned.

When I arrived at the campus I started hunting around for the props I needed. But wouldn't you know it, this was a modern campus—it looked identical to every other rural college, and there were no miners to be seen anywhere. Only regular-looking students were in the halls of the student union. But I had this brilliant skit to perform, and I needed the props.

"Listen," I told the boy in the student activities office. "I have an idea for a skit to start the show, but I need a couple of miner's caps with lamps."

He gave me a blank stare.

"What kind of caps?"

"You know, like coal miners wear."

"Hmmm . . ."

They had T-shirts, movie passes, lab coats, sweat-shirts, umbrellas, lollipops, and candy kisses . . . but the boy said, "I'm afraid we don't have miner's caps. And I haven't the foggiest notion where I could even begin to hunt something like that down."

Suddenly I realized that although the school was *called* Mines, it didn't necessarily mean that it was filled with coal miners, and it also didn't mean that students were required to purchase miner's caps for their laboratory classes. Nevertheless, my heart was set on this skit and I decided to do everything in my power to make it happen.

"What about an overhead projector?" I asked.

"I can get my hands on one of those."

"Great."

"I'll be right back with it—"

"One more thing before you go."

"Yes?"

"Can the room lights be killed?"

He walked to the back of the theater where the show was scheduled, and he hit the light switches one by one until we were plunged into total darkness.

"Perfect."

He disappeared to get the overhead projector, and I went through my sound check. While I was doing that, I surveyed the venue: for all intents and purposes, it might have been a small movie theater. There was a raised stage up front, and the room was about thirty by fifty feet. The only difference was that the seats were folding chairs, not fixed chairs like in a movie theater. While I was arranging things to my liking, the first two volunteers arrived. The girl was an attractive blonde and she was wearing a denim miniskirt. This couple would be the center of attention, I knew, but her outfit wouldn't work for this show, especially if I chose them to be the miner couple.

"I'm glad you arrived early," I said. "I appreciate the fact that you dressed nice for the performance, too, but I should have told the school that a number of the kissing demonstrations involve moving into positions where you might want to be wearing a longer skirt, or even pants. For instance, there's one scene in the dentist office where the boy falls to the floor and you tackle him. And there's another scene I'd like you guys to do in a mine shaft."

"Oh," she said.

Her boyfriend nodded.

"Do you live nearby?" I asked.

"Yes, in the dorm," the girl said.

"Okay, after the rehearsal, which we're going to start momentarily, you can decide if you want to run back and do a quick change."

Three other couples had moseyed into the theater, and I took everyone into the student activities office to rehearse. The guy running the show had borrowed two bicycle helmets that we could use in place of miner's caps. I thought it was ironic that I was at the Colorado School of Mines and they didn't have authentic miner's caps, but I put that thought out of my head and focused on making the opening of the show work. We rehearsed the scene with the lights on, but I warned the couple that during the show the lights would be off, and the only illumination would be provided by an overhead projector.

That's how we left it, and then we finished rehearsing the rest of the show.

After rehearsal the girl vanished, and for a while I was nervous that she and her boyfriend might have decided at the last minute to drop out. Then I wouldn't have a couple for the miners skit. The theater was filled with kids, and they seemed to be in a serious mood. I didn't realize it at the time, but Mines has one of the most academically accomplished groups of students in the United States. Some of the students had books with them, and compared with other schools, it was an intellectual-looking group. I was fuming at the way Kevin had misled me, convinced that this audience was going to be a tough sell.

I seated three couples on stage, but the lead couple's seats were still empty. It was already eight minutes past the scheduled start time, and the student in charge wanted to introduce me. I gave him the go-ahead. Just as we were about to start, the girl and her boyfriend ducked down and slipped into their chairs onstage. She had changed into blue jeans, and I breathed a sigh of relief. Now all I had to do was direct the miners skit and hope against hope that this crowd would lighten up and come out of their studious attitude.

"It's a pleasure to be here at the Colorado School of Mines," I began. "You have such a romantic campus. There are so many nice places around here to kiss." Then I mentioned a few locations at their school that I had learned from talking with my demonstrators. In actuality *none* of these locations were romantic, and this elicited a few laughs. With that auspicious beginning, I launched into my new skit.

"Because we're doing this show at Mines, we thought it only fitting to show you a scene that happened not long ago when two students became lost in a deep mine shaft. In your mind's eye I want you to picture a boy and girl who are trapped a hundred feet underground."

I signaled the light man, and the room was plunged into darkness. A moment later he switched on the overhead projector. I had covered it with aluminum foil, leaving only a narrow slit for the light. On cue, the girl knelt at one end of the stage, her boyfriend at the other. They looked like lost miners! Slowly they began crawling toward each other. The light beam intermittently shone over the boy's shoulder, as if coming from a miner's lamp. Now and then it illuminated the girl, and there were gasps of excitement from the audience.

"They're drawing closer!" I cried. "Remember, they're lovers. They've been trapped underground and separated for days, without even knowing if their partner was dead or alive . . . Suddenly the girl spies a light up ahead. She crawls forward with hope rising in her heart."

Now the two kids were within ten feet of one another, their hands on the floor, their faces raised, peering into the obscurity. That's when I delivered the punchline.

"The girl gives a shout of joy. She recognizes her boyfriend. They've found each other at last! They hear the pickaxes of their rescuers breaking through the collapsed mine. They put their lips together for a first romantic kiss—deep in that mine shaft."

Illuminated by a beam of yellow, the two demonstrators kissed.

"Later that year," I continued, "they became the first two students to graduate from the Colorado School of Mines."

This conclusion got a big laugh. The house lights came up, and I was able to direct the rest of the show and connect fairly well with the engineering students, even though they still had a more serious disposition than most other audiences. At least I had demonstrated a good-faith effort to get to know something about their school, which is always appreciated by college students. They're proud of where they're learning, they have school spirit, and if you can genuinely say something nice about the place where you're speaking, it goes a long way toward winning an audience's trust and goodwill.

CHAPTER THIRTY-ONE

AMERICAN GIRLS

AT THE AGE OF THIRTEEN I MADE A PROMISE
to myself that I'm proud to say I've kept. Sitting in the back
of my high school English class, I started daydreaming
about my future, and although I wasn't particularly
athletic or musically inclined, all I had to do was look
around at the careers of athletes and rock stars to realize
that most of them hit their peak during their twenties and
thirties. Did I want a career that fizzled out before half
my life was over? At the same time, I had just learned that
Sophocles continued writing prize-winning plays into his
nineties. That's when I decided to try for a writing career.

But I never imagined that my first book would become
an international best-seller or that it would lead to my
directing a live show. Trust me, I never sought this kind
of life, I never thought it would suit me, and I never imagined that droves of girls would show up to watch me direct
kissing demonstrations. But, friends, I'm only human, and
when my writing career—which was supposed to be quiet
and solitary, with me sitting at a desk in a remote cabin,
like Thoreau—took me into the world of live performing,
and when college girls started showing up and screaming

in near-hysterical frenzy at my kissing shows, and when they started coming into my dressing room and trying to get together with me, I must have lost my mind, because I broke down and did a lot of stupid things.

At first I couldn't believe what was happening. I mean, when three hundred girls were nearly jumping out of their seats at a small college, and then when they came up afterward and started flirting with me, it never occurred to me that it was real. I thought they were joking around. But after this happened seventy or eighty times, I guess I got careless and I began to slip into that fantasy world where I imagined I was a rock star too, especially because an over-the-top audience reaction can seduce you into thinking that you're someone you're not.

"Is it the applause that's making you introduce spanking skits into the class?" Father Woods asked.

He was referring to the applause I got on the road. Father was a very insightful guy.

People often ask whether I've been pursued by groupies. Believe it or not, the answer is yes, but in my case they weren't usually like rock 'n' roll groupies; my fans turned out to be bookish and even nerdy types. One girl contacted me after reading my book and described herself as voluptuous. That in and of itself didn't impress me. What *did* impress me was her tenacity: she kept calling, emailing, and sending letters and cards. When you're on the road it can get lonely, and if a girl throws herself at you it's tempting to start a relationship, if only to stave off that feeling of emptiness that creeps in when you leave a venue late at night and have the prospect of facing a cold and impersonal airport in the morning. So when this girl, whose name was Amanda Janson, told me that she was going to drive a hundred miles to meet me after a show at James Madison University in Harrisonburg, Virginia, I started to get a little nervous. But I had no one I could ask for advice.

Are you some kind of blockhead? you may be asking. *Can't you seek advice from your psychotherapist or your minister?*

Now, that might work for most people, but you have to remember that my father administered so many psychological tests to me when I was a youngster that I rebelled against the entire field of psychology, and by the age of nine I had zero faith in it—I refused to see a psychoanalyst for any reason, unable to believe they could do me any good. I also rejected my family's religion, Catholicism, and tried Buddhism instead, but I lost interest in that after I started feeling lethargic from meditating. So I had no professional or religious people I trusted to tell me what I should do about this girl who was coming to see me.

Don't laugh, but I did develop a pen-pal friendship with a girl from Texas who read my book, and I decided to ask *her* for advice. She lived in Laredo, which is close to Mexico. I know what you're thinking: How can a girl you've never met give you relationship advice? You're an author, you should be giving *her* advice, not the other way around. But my mind doesn't work like that; instead, I figured that she was a girl, she knew what girls were like better than I did, and she could tell me what Amanda Janson really wanted. So I called my Texan friend.

"I'm right in the middle of watching a movie," she said. "But hold on a second."

In the background I could hear the dialogue of the film stop midstream. When she got back on the line she asked me how I was, and I brought her up to date about my problem with this girl planning to drive hundreds of miles to visit me.

"Oh, don't worry about it," she said.

"But what does she want?"

"She just wants to meet you."

"That's all?"

"I think she must kind of idolize you."

"Should I take her to dinner?" I said. I appreciated any advice she could give—she was so savvy about relationships.

"Most definitely."

"Okay, pussycat, thanks!"

I called her pussycat for laughs. She went back to her movie, and I got ready for my trip to Harrisonburg. During the performance I started getting nervous because I didn't know if my admirer was in the audience or not, but after I got offstage and started packing up my props, a thin girl with short black hair and dark eyes approached me.

"Hi, I'm Amanda Janson."

Even though she was friendly, I was still nervous.

"I like the name Amanda," I said.

"Oh, it's a fake name," she said. "My real name is—" I can't even remember it now, it was such an unusual name.

I gave her a quizzical look.

She blushed and said, "Oh, I lied to you about a lot of things. I didn't describe myself truthfully. I claimed I had an hourglass figure. I gave you a false name. I claimed I read books I never read."

"Hey, don't worry about it," I said.

"But I thought you'd want to meet me more if I was voluptuous."

"Listen, that doesn't matter to me."

"No?"

"All I care about is what kind of a person you are inside, you know? It doesn't even bother me if you never read *The Conspiracy Against the Human Race* . . . You didn't, did you? Well, okay, that *does* bother me. No, I'm kidding! Cheer up. It's okay, really it is. But never mind about that stuff, you know, I just wanted to meet you."

She looked like she was about to melt, she was so happy. But I didn't know what I was saying. I don't know what rock musicians feel like when groupies visit them in their dressing room and want to start a relationship, but that's the kind of pressure I felt. I was wondering how I could get out of there as quickly as possible, but without hurting this girl's feelings. After all, she had driven a hundred miles to see me, if what she told me was true.

So I took my Texan friend's advice and bought the girl a soda and pizza, and then when she was getting ready to leave, I felt that I owed her some token of affection, and I took her out to the parking lot and gave her a simple little lip kiss. If that kiss had appeared in my show, nobody would have screamed and jumped out of their seat. But it was a personal statement and it meant something to her and me, so I have no qualms about it. When she left, I started thinking about that promise I had made to myself when I was thirteen, the promise to become a writer because it was so unlike the life of a rock star and it was unlikely to fizzle out. If this kind of thing kept happening, I realized, my life of quiet solitude might never come to fruition. I made a vow to try and avoid these kinds of meetings in the future, or at least to try and get a girl who liked to read philosophy.

Wouldn't you know it, but shortly thereafter a beautiful Mexican girl began sending me photos of herself. When I saw the first photo I thought it was an advertisement for a dating site. The girl was wearing a pair of blue jeans, and she looked like she was in her early twenties. She had extremely long black hair, a beautiful smile, and pretty eyes. When I started getting these emails, I really didn't know what to do. At first I simply deleted the images, thinking she must have copied them from a fashion magazine. But one day I happened to mull over the subject line: *From a beautiful girl to the author of The Art of Kissing.* How could a person who was falsifying her identity know that I wrote a book? People who perpetrate international frauds don't usually research their potential victims. I clicked open the email and read the message. Unknown to me, doing that was going to change my life in a most uncomfortable way.

The girl really was from Mexico, and she wanted to get to know me better, so to humor her I started communicating with her by email. I figured I could say a few nice things and get her off my back, but I had no idea how these things work, how they can progress without your even being aware of what's happening, and how they can quickly tie you into a knot. She started to respond to my polite notes with increasing frequency, and in her replies she revealed that she was a lawyer. Then she mentioned that it was very dangerous to live in Mexico. If you've read Roberto Bolaño's *2666*, that section of the book with all the murders of young women, you know how frighteningly true this was. This girl's name was Arcelia, and she told me that she wanted to emigrate to another country. Meanwhile, I had been collecting scores of poems from her, each more difficult to understand than the next since they were half in English and half in Spanish. She really was quite intelligent and could easily have been an up-and-coming young poet in Mexico or even in the United States.

Eventually, she started calling me, and our second conversation went like this. (See if you can spot where I made my big mistake.)

"I like you," she said.

"I like you," I replied.

That's not the mistake—it gets worse.

"Do you think we're compatible?" she asked.

I'm thinking: *Compatible?* What is she asking me that for? Isn't that something you ask when you're contemplating a relationship?

"Oh, sure," I lied.

For one thing, she had such a thick accent I couldn't understand most of what she said. For another, she was a lawyer and I was a lawyer, and I found most lawyers boring. I didn't want to be in a relationship with a lawyer. So I didn't think we were too compatible. And third, she kept sending me complicated romantic poems about herself, and I had so little command of the Spanish language that I couldn't bring myself to delete them from my computer because I thought that maybe they were about me, and maybe someday I'd be able to understand them. It was nerve-racking to get them and to think this girl was foisting herself on me. But how can you argue with a girl who's going out of her way to be nice to you? When I was thirteen, remember, I had selected a career that was solitary and insular, and I didn't invite this kind of attention.

Then she suddenly came out with this question:

"Do you want to marry me?"

"*What!*"

"Do you want to marry me?"

"Marry you?"

"Did I insult you?"

"No, no, no, dear." I was already calling her *dear*! "No, you didn't insult me."

"You don't want to marry me?"

"No, not at all. I mean, err, sure, okay, I'll marry you." Suddenly her tone changed and she became excited.

"You will?"

"Sure," I said.

It was a joke, right? We were thousands of miles apart. I figured a little flirting on the phone couldn't hurt.

Not realizing that she was dead serious, I had said "Sure" to her marriage question, and before I knew it I was engaged. Future conversations and emails all contained reassurances that she would see me soon and that we would live happily ever after. She even started discussing how many kids she wanted to have. It was only years later that I realized how desperately she wanted to get out of the country and that she saw me as a good way of accomplishing her goal.

A few weeks later, at a conference in Lancaster, Pennsylvania, I told my agent that I was engaged. Kevin just laughed.

"No, you're not," he said.

He thought I was working on a stand-up routine. But the truth is that I had inadvertently become engaged to this woman. The only thing that saved me was that she met a new pen pal from Italy and flew to Rome to meet him and fell head over heels in love and married the Italian guy. I was narrowly saved from a life with a woman I couldn't understand and who was absolutely the wrong type of person for me. The sad truth is that if she hadn't met the guy from Italy, I probably would have kept my word and married her, that's the kind of dolt I am.

I tried to have a solitary writing life, but like I said, the kissing show changed all that. Before I knew what was happening, girls were coming out of the woodwork and making my life not exactly miserable, but certainly very different. After the show became popular, girls would often come up to me after the performance for a kiss. They wanted to boast to their friends that they had kissed the man who wrote the book on kissing. If I didn't like them I claimed that my contract prohibited it, but I rarely had to invoke the contract clause.

CHAPTER THIRTY-TWO

IDAHO
STATE UNIVERSITY

I HAD ONE FINAL KILLER SHOW ON SEPTEMBER 15, 2000, before everything fell apart. It's indelibly impressed upon my memory precisely because it was the last all-out good time the kissing show produced for a college audience before budget-conscious administrators and consciousness-raising protesters shut the door forever on one of the most successful presentations to hit the college lecture circuit. And it happened in, of all places, Idaho.

Every time I ventured into the great Northwest I would gird my loins for what I considered a solitary and lonely adventure. I'm not talking about the colleges—they were exciting and fun—but the physical environment in which they were situated was something else. There was the incessant fog of Seattle, the semiarid desert of Yakima Valley, the sublime views of snow-capped Mount Rainier, and the overwhelming sense of isolation—all of which had to be transmuted by eight o'clock in the evening into a rollicking good time for the students at my show. But at Idaho State University I was so close to the wilderness of the great Northwest—Yellowstone National Park, the foothills of the Rockies, and rafting and fishing country—that I didn't know if I was going to be able to dredge up enough good cheer to bring the show alive for kids who I suspected would have come from farm and ranch families and whose pastimes probably included attending rodeos and hunting quail. I was having a nightmare as my flight into Pocatello Regional Airport was delayed out of Chicago. I kept checking my watch, glaring at the rain, and cursing cruel fate, which always pushed me to a near nervous condition every time I was late for a show. I was going to be late arriving for this one, no question about it. The way things were going, I might even miss it.

By the time I arrived in Pocatello and was picked up by the two kids from the campus activities board, I was a wreck. There would be no time for rehearsal. There would be no time for sound check. There would be no time for anything but disaster. I gritted my teeth and tried not to let my disappointment come across to these kids. Here I was in a beautiful part of the country and it was already dark, so I wasn't going to see a blasted thing except the inside of a university auditorium. I had a sinking feeling that nobody was going to come to the event.

But on that score I couldn't have been more wrong. The two kids led me into the venue, a low-ceilinged cafeteria, and it was packed with people—all of whom had been waiting for nearly half an hour for me to arrive.

"We made an announcement that the show was delayed due to your flight out of Chicago," the student in charge of the event said.

As soon as I walked into the cafeteria, I sized up the situation as a disaster in the making. Yes, there were four couples waiting for me to direct them, and there were three hundred kids waiting to see the show . . . but without a sound check and rehearsal, what would they be getting? I was afraid that they wouldn't be getting the full experience, and I was thinking dreary thoughts, such as: *They're being robbed of the finest performance I can give them, and they don't even know it.* So the first thing I did was grab the microphone and talk to the students. I needed to connect with them immediately, apologize for the unavoidable delay, and get a sense of how they were feeling.

"I'm so sorry about the flight delay," I began. They were sitting scattered around the cafeteria. I walked into the crowd and continued talking to them, making eye contact with boys and girls who all looked like terrifically nice people. "Listen, I have to ask you an important question. I know we're already twenty minutes past the scheduled start time, but do you want me to rehearse, like I usually do, or would you like us to just get the demonstrators in their places and wing it, doing the entire show unrehearsed?"

There was an amazing surge of energy in response to that question.

"Let's start now!"

"No rehearsal!"

"Go, go, go!"

"Yaaaaaaaay!"

I smiled to myself. In the middle of the Idaho night—nestled between some of the biggest national forests in the country—I had hit upon a pocket of electric excitement and energy, and it was right here, right now, in this room! Encouraged by this energy and love that I felt coming from these kids, all of whom were polite but also super charged up with anticipation and excitement, I felt a positive mandate to go forward. So I put the best face on it that I could, knowing in my heart of hearts that by not rehearsing I was risking giving them a disaster. I tried to think positive thoughts, for myself and for *them*.

"Well, stand by, folks—give me just two minutes and I'll get my demonstrators in place. But the good news is that without a rehearsal you're going to see some of the most exciting boy-girl interactions you'll ever witness, because each and every kiss will be a *first* kiss, with all the sensual energy that entails. I'll be with you in two shakes of a lamb's tail. And during that time, folks, I suggest that you drag your chairs closer to us, and what we'll do—if you're willing—is we'll present the program right down here on the floor, giving each and every one of you a much more intimate view. If we do it in the round, it's going to be like you're at a party when the lights are shut off and people start making out. You're going to be right up close and personal with the kissers. Are you up for that?"

"Yaaaaaay!"

"Let's do it!"

"Yo-yo-yo-yo-yo-yo-yo!"

I wheeled to my demonstrators and motioned them to approach, already starting to sweat with anxiety and with the added exertion this show was going to demand. I quickly took eight folding chairs off the makeshift stage and brought them down to the floor, arranging them in a circle facing the crowd. And I motioned for the demonstrators to approach me.

"Listen," I said. "We have no time to rehearse, so it's critically important that you do one thing, and one thing only—*listen* to my voice. I'll have the microphone, so you'll always be able to hear me. But I want you to *ignore* the crowd, *ignore* any screams and yells you hear from them. Don't talk to your partner—it will interfere with the show and make the audience think they're missing a line of dialogue. Instead, be silent and listen for my voice coming through the chaos and confusion that's going to happen tonight. Believe me when I say that I'll be talking directly to each of you, and I'll be giving you specific directions on exactly what to do. Don't worry, it won't be anything embarrassing, but you must follow my directions to the letter for the show to work, okay? Have faith in me. I've directed it literally hundreds of times, and I know it will work. You're with me, right?"

These eight kids looked at me like they were standing on the edge of a sheer cliff and I was asking them to jump off—and in a way, that's exactly what I was asking.

One of the boys was short and handsome, and his girlfriend was a cute brunette. This boy gave me a wry look, and I worried that he would challenge me during the show. When you have an unrehearsed guy who rebels and thinks it's funny to fight against the person who's directing, it's a sure recipe for a ruined performance. I knew I needed to keep him on my side. His girlfriend wouldn't be a problem, but *he* might. I also realized that if I could win *him* over, that is, if I could make him feel comfortable enough to go along with all my skits— including the spanking kiss, the vacuum kiss, and the car kiss at the end—then everybody *else* in the show would do a fine job and generally follow his lead. With this in mind, I placed the demonstrators in their seats facing the crowd, and then I turned to the audience and made my final plea, inviting them to pull their chairs up even closer.

"You'll have a better view, trust me, and I won't call on anybody who's in the first three rows." My standard line worked like a charm, and almost all three hundred of them hiked their chairs closer to us.

And then I got into it, putting every bit of my experience with hundreds of audiences and thousands of volunteers into play, tapping all that previous success to guide these eight demonstrators into the performance of their lives. The audience was so close I could smell the garlic on their breath from their dinners, and when I ran around my volunteers in their 360-degree setup, I was brushing past the pant legs and skirts of the boys and girls sitting in the first row.

I pushed fast into my opening jokes, truncating the routine as I sensed the pulse of the audience waxing and waning with me. I didn't use all my quotations, only the most effective ones, and I listened for their laughter— when it was good, I slowed down and relaxed a bit; when it wasn't good, I moved ahead more quickly. When you're only two feet from an audience, so close that you're accidentally stepping on their shoes, you can unintentionally intimidate them, and it requires a heightened sensitivity to their feelings to make it work. Eye contact is a key, but you can't stare at someone too long or they'll feel intimidated; just *enough* eye contact is what it takes, but not too much. I was pacing myself, moving quicker than usual for a college show, but also keeping a careful eye on my eight volunteers. I had to keep them happy above everything else—especially that guy who might buck and run like a wild boar if I didn't make him feel comfortable.

And then the fireworks started happening. I sensed

that the audience had gotten over their annoyance with the late start, and I could feel them following me with each transition from kiss to kiss and skit to skit. Everything was working precisely the way I wanted it to, and even the guy I had handed the music cue sheet to without rehearsal was staying with me so that the soundtrack was adding to the momentum of the show. At this point we came to the neck kiss, and I was worried that the key couple would rebel and not make the switch. Remember, I hadn't prepared them for it, I hadn't even mentioned it beforehand. But when I reached the point for the switcheroo, the crowd was laughing so much that the guy shot an inquisitive *Okay, honey?* glance at his girl, and then he moved to the next chair and knelt down—and at my cue he miraculously kissed the new girl's neck. The audience cheered, and at the next switch more magic happened: while making the move to the next chair, one of the guys lost his balance and accidentally slipped off the girl he was kissing and fell onto the floor. He had the most wonderful smile on his face as this happened, and two feet behind him the people in the audience were dying with laughter. It was a special moment—but it was going to get even better.

I must pause here to comment that one of the pleasures of doing a show with no rehearsal or sound check is that the protesters don't have a chance to sink their fangs into you. You slip past all that nonsense and connect directly with the audience. There was no pall hanging over our heads. It was just us in that room having fun—almost like a bunch of kids in a playground when your parents aren't looking.

Now I was approaching the finale, the all-important

car skit, which would be the last image we would leave in the minds of this audience way out here in the American wilderness. I wanted the challenging guy to participate fully, so I set the skit up by helping each couple move into the proper position, with the guys keeping their hands up on the wheels, and then I stepped close to my key performer and whispered, "You can do this!" It seemed to give him the encouragement he needed, and he focused on holding his hands on the steering wheel, simulating driving down the highway.

I sprang to the edge of the demonstrators' circle and faced the audience, simultaneously barking instructions into the microphone for the volunteers:

"The girl is trying to make you have an accident. *She climbs up onto your lap.* Watch out for that truck! Downshift! Downshift!"

I spun to check my demonstrators. All of them, including my key couple, were in perfect sync. It looked lovely the way the brunette had climbed up onto her boyfriend's lap, and I launched into my final instruction.

"He raises one hand *high* off the wheel—!" I raised one of my hands, and all four guys followed my lead, raising one hand behind the girls. The choreography was clicking, the volume of the music rose on cue, the audience leaned forward, and I said, "He begins spanking her as she kisses him. *Spank* that girl! . . . *Kiss* that boy! . . . And *this*, my friends, is American kissing at its best!"

Let me tell you that when those four couples all did that skit at the same time, just inches from the audience, it had to be the most thrilling moment of my college lecture career. The bliss of not having anyone protesting or trying to disrupt the performance was a big part of the success of that show, but more than anything it was the benign smile of old mother fate taking a hand in making it all turn out right. She had stepped out of the inky black wilderness of the American Northwest and lent us a helping hand.

You can't ask for more than that.

CHAPTER THIRTY-THREE

WEST COAST COLLEGES

THE FIRST TIME I TRAVELED TO WASHINGTON, a woman picked me up in a Jeep. She wore a white shift dress and had long red hair. Up and down the mountains we roared in her Jeep, and I had a feeling that I was being whisked into another world.

The student union resembled a barnwood-paneled hunting lodge. The roof was crisscrossed by heavy wooden trusses, and a hundred folding chairs stood awaiting an audience. After my sound check the director of student activities showed me the upstairs level, which had a huge fireplace and wall-to-wall carpet, and it was vacant so we would have it all to ourselves for rehearsal. The demonstrators were fine young students who seemed excited about being in the production.

When we returned to the venue after rehearsal about fifty people had arrived. They were in a good mood. The audience struck me as less uptight than at East Coast schools. People were still coming into the room, and they looked eager to see the performance. But they didn't have that stressed and hyped-up energy you get from New York and Pennsylvania crowds. I also had time to go over my music cues, and luckily the student in charge of that seemed to be competent.

"I've been on the road for two months this semester," I began. "And I feel like I'm going to give you the best performance of my career." I had stolen that line from my friend Chance Langton, and the audience could see that I had slipped into a West Coast frame of mind: relaxed, easygoing, friendly. As the show progressed the sun set and the floor-to-ceiling windows behind the stage darkened and became reflective. I went off my prearranged set list and included the mirror kiss, a scenario where two people smooch in front of a wall mirror. My demonstrators gamely played along. Such a delightful group.

A few weeks later I performed at another school in the state, and the energy was a little higher. The venue was a narrow room that had been painted royal blue. At this school the demonstrators, eight upperclassmen, were more experienced. They had an edgy vitality and energy that spilled over into their kisses. The audience reacted with loud cheers and good-natured yells. I felt very comfortable with this crowd because they weren't annoying and they didn't talk over my narration, unlike some hecklers I had encountered in other parts of the country.

In the back of the venue a college dispensary sold snacks, beer, and wine. Many of the students at this late-night event were drinking, but again, it didn't negatively impact their behavior. On the East Coast this kind of setup could pose a problem, considering that those New England and Middle Atlantic students tended to become undisciplined when they drank. I'm not sure how or why West Coast kids managed to handle their liquor so well, but they certainly did, and I finished the show with a wonderfully positive feeling about them.

After the performance I walked back toward my motel along a college pathway, and the sound of crickets and the deep darkness of the pine trees struck me as a stark contrast to the bright and boisterous interior of that performance hall. I suddenly felt a sharp letdown. It had been the last show of the semester, and it was now over: the cheering and applause were gone, the smiling girls and fun-loving guys were nowhere to be seen, and I was alone in a place where I didn't know anyone.

I started to think about the strange way things had been going over the past few years. Audiences almost always enjoyed the show, but a handful of feminist and lesbian protesters had had an inordinate impact on sales. Despite the fact that the performance overwhelmingly appealed to girls and despite our open policy on same-sex couples, Kevin had warned me that the lecture circuit was becoming so politically correct that even acts like Chris Rock and Jerry Seinfeld had decided not to do college shows anymore. Another problem that cut into our popularity was how burgeoning internet and cell phone usage had slowly but surely eroded attendance at lectures.

What did it all mean? Why was I still doing kissing shows? How had my simple plan to be a writer, formulated at age thirteen, turned into this experience? Was I destined to be on the lecture circuit forever even as the political climate at colleges was changing? And what about the fact that the show had been criticized by protesting students at some schools? Did I really have to be concerned about that, as Kevin suggested? Was he right in telling me that it was the beginning of the end?

Many other lecture agents, he said, were also complaining about decreasing sales as a result of the changing political feelings on college campuses and the way the internet was reducing audience sizes at live events.

I have one final West Coast school to tell you about, and it was one of my favorites: Santa Clara University in San Jose, California. This was the most picturesque campus I ever visited. The buildings reflected the influences of Spanish and Mexican architecture, with low single- and two-story structures, arched passageways, and cloistered walks. The grounds sprawled green and spacious, and the students were friendly and outgoing. They invited me to present the kissing show three times, and once I also did a new show about birth order directly after the kissing program. The birth order show was all about how your siblings impact your personality and romantic compatibility.

Audra Lee was the student in charge of the event. She was nineteen and had black hair and intelligent eyes. She also had a can-do attitude that helped things go smoothly. Of all the thousands of students that I met during my trips to colleges across the country, the only one that I kept in contact with after the show was Audra. She loved to read and wanted to be a writer, and she always had a good list of books to recommend.

The Santa Clara venue was adjacent to a bar, and the students drank before, during, and after the show, but for some reason it never became a problem like it did at East Coast schools. As in Washington State, these youngsters knew how to have fun without becoming obstreperous. Their stage was flanked on either side by towering loudspeakers. The room held three hundred, and each time we came out of rehearsal the place was completely packed.

I think I encountered more couples in the audience at Santa Clara than anywhere else. There were plenty of single girls too, and many of them crowded close to the footlights, but there were also West Coast beachcomber guys with blond hair and their girlfriends standing along the outskirts of the crowd, sitting high up on the wall near the entrance, and congregating near the bar. One of the most successful skits for this crowd was the spanking kiss, where I had the boys playfully spank their partners during a lip kiss. But in an inspired moment, I ad-libbed and asked the audience whether they would also like to see the girls spank the boys.

"Hell yes!"

"Pleeeeeeeeease!"

"Yaaaaaaaay!"

I hadn't prepared my demonstrators, but they went along with it. The girls raised their hands high and at my cue brought them down in a loud *spank*! One of the boys yelped and jumped clear off the platform, at which point the house erupted in laughter. Before the show, Audra had informed me that this boy had been matched with one of the girls from the student activities board. His girlfriend couldn't make it, but she had told him that she didn't want him doing the show without her. We were supposed to keep it quiet and not announce that he was kissing a new girl without his girlfriend's permission—but apparently word had spread through the audience and everyone was aware of the situation. The boy looked highly embarrassed when they started laughing at him, but I think he was more worried that his girlfriend would find out. Still, he decided to take the risk, and before long he was doing the demonstrations with uninhibited abandon.

When all's said and done, West Coast schools embodied the spirit of American romance so perfectly that I was sorry every time I had to depart from their campuses. I know that some of the students who attended my shows eventually moved to other parts of the country, even other parts of the world, and I feel proud to have shared this production with them, especially since I'm sure that after they graduated they took that laid-back West Coast attitude to heart—along with some of the romantic tips and tricks from the kissing show.

CHAPTER THIRTY-FOUR

KISSING LESSONS

"WHEN IS YOUR NEXT KISSING CLASS?"

The caller was a young woman.

"Let me explain," I said. "There are no *classes* per se, you understand?"

"Oh, no? But my husband and I need—"

"Don't worry. The lessons are *private*."

"You mean it's just the two of us?"

"Precisely."

"Great! When can we book it?"

After I moved to New York City in 2001, I started receiving calls like this from women who wanted to attend my kissing classes. How did they get it into their heads that I offered classes? The answer is rather amusing. But first I wish to provide the context in which these private lessons originated.

On the morning of September 11, 2001, I was in the gym with about ten other people on the fiftieth floor of my apartment building on Fifty-Seventh Street in Manhattan, and we watched in horror as those tragic events unfolded before our eyes. The Contemporary Issues Agency was lucky not to have anyone in the air on that day, but for months and years afterward we experienced a precipitous drop in bookings. This decline affected our entire industry, including hundreds of college agencies. Combined with the increased number of protesters and the changed political climate on college campuses, this downturn in bookings spelled the end for the kissing show. The last one I directed was on February 20, 2012, at Ohio University in Athens, Ohio. Close to two hundred students attended, and they loved it. I still traveled on the college circuit but after that I lectured about birth order, and I had another show on subliminal advertising, which I called the Wilson Bryan Key Memorial Lecture in memory of my friend, who died in 2008.

With that as the backdrop, we can return to those private kissing lessons. It all started the day a New York television station decided to film a segment on kissing. The producer wanted to shoot it in Central Park, and she asked whether I knew anyone who would be willing to appear on the program. She certainly asked the right guy—I knew scores of young people who were dying for media attention. They were all New York actors.

New York City is replete with people who want to make it big in the world of entertainment. I think there must be more aspiring actors in Manhattan than anywhere else on earth except Hollywood. Indeed, one of the main reasons I moved to the Big Apple was to do television and theater productions, and I immediately set about holding auditions on Forty-Second Street. My ad in *Backstage* drew hundreds of young actors, and I cast them in readings, plays, musicals, and local television shows. So when this producer asked whether I could find a few people, I smiled to myself. These actors were hungry for television experience, and they jumped at the opportunity. Twenty of these young hopefuls showed up at the Central Park fountain on the day of the shoot, and the producer was in seventh heaven. Not only were these volunteers young and good-looking, they also had exactly the kind of discipline that producers loved: they stood where you wanted them to stand, they moved the way you asked them to move, and they kissed on cue. Joe Whelski, for example, went out in a rowboat on the Central Park lake with Melissa Bowman, and at a prearranged signal they stopped rowing and started kissing. Their romantic smooch provided a lovely establishing shot.

After we had the exteriors finished, eight actors accompanied me to my apartment on the twentieth floor on Fifty-Seventh Street, and the producer shot a kissing class during which I coached the attendees as if they were real couples. Joanne Dalton, a tall actress whom we had cast earlier in the year as my nurse in a television comedy, appeared as one of the girls in the kissing class. On cue, these young people did neck kisses, sliding kisses, and even french kisses for the camera. A few weeks later they were rewarded when the segment appeared on television. I don't know if the program resulted in any of them landing extra acting jobs, but it sure looked good on their résumés. In the following months, Joe Whelski worked with me on a number of other kissing projects, and even though he was married, he received permission from his wife to kiss Brittney Houseman, another New York actress. Together, the three of us did television and live presentations for a consumer goods company, which had engaged my services to publicize a new beauty bar.

Once I uploaded some photos of the kissing program

to my website, I started getting calls from women asking when they could enroll with their husbands and boyfriends in the kissing classes.

"I'm afraid that you're under the mistaken impression that I conduct an ongoing class to teach you how to kiss," I told them. "But I have an even better deal for you—a private lesson. It'll last two hours, during which you and your inamorata will have my undivided attention. The two of you will learn all you need to know about how to kiss romantically. We'll go over thirty kisses from my book, and I guarantee that all your questions will be answered during this lesson."

"Oh, yes, I want it!"

Now the funny thing is that single women started calling me too. The typical caller said the reason she needed a lesson was because she was a bad kisser.

"And what makes you think you're a bad kisser?" I would ask.

The answer was invariably the same: "My boyfriend made a comment that I'm no good." Or perhaps it was the ex-boyfriend, and the girl was devastated by this criticism. One thing I learned right away from doing the lessons with couples was that while men were self-focused and overconfident about their abilities, including their kissing abilities, women were much more other-focused and concerned with pleasing their partners, so much so that they often totally ignored their own pleasure and considered their own satisfaction to be of insignificant value. The number one thing I had to teach men was to stop being egocentric and try to understand what their partner might like. And the number one lesson women needed to learn—including all the single girls who wanted help—was that they had to stop trying so hard to please the boys and start making sure that *they* were enjoying the experience of kissing and making out.

But what was I to do for these unfortunate young women who had no partner, or who were so unsure of their kissing abilities that they sought a secret kissing lesson without their boyfriend's knowledge? The first girl to show up for a private lesson without a partner asked if I would simply talk to her and, if necessary, kiss her, to teach her what to do. When she appeared on a spring day in Central Park for her lesson, I was astounded to see that she was exceptionally attractive. I was sure that any young man would be happy to kiss her. I told her as much, but this didn't improve her confidence. Then I explained that I considered it unethical for me to kiss her, but that I would coach her for an hour and make sure that she improved her self-confidence. In other words, right at the outset I gave her a pep talk to try and build up her confidence. Then I tried to find out exactly what she needed from the lesson.

"What's the main thing you want to learn?"

"I need to find out how to kiss a boy."

"Yes, but, I mean, is there anything specific you want to work on today?"

"Maybe how to use my tongue?"

"Do boys use their tongue with you a lot?"

"Oh, all the time."

"I see."

"That's the first thing they do."

"I see."

"They stick their tongue in and I—well, I don't know what to do because."

"Why not?"

"Because I choke, or I can't breathe."

Now, friends, in *The Art of Kissing* I explain quite clearly that the number one mistake guys make is that they do french kisses too soon in a relationship and they stick their tongues too far down the girl's throat so that she can't breathe. Standing before me was proof positive of that irrefutable kissing statistic.

"Young lady, the problem isn't with you," I told her. "It's with your boyfriends."

"It is?"

"It's these guys who don't know how to kiss."

"Are you sure?"

"Haven't I surveyed more than a hundred thousand people all across the United States?"

"But they seem to think they're doing it right—"

"That's because guys are self-centered. And also because you, as a girl, are too other-focused, too intent on trying to please these guys."

"But what should I do when the tongue comes in? I mean, they push their tongues in so fast and hard, I start to gag."

"There are three things you can do. And I'm telling you this based on the experience of thousands of girls. First of all, you have to realize that no matter how big or strong a boy is—even if he's as tough as Mike Tyson—his soft little tongue is no match for your teeth. Do I make myself clear?"

"My *teeth*?"

"All you have to do is bite down—gently, at first; more insistently, if necessary—into his intrusive and annoying little tongue, and that boy will quickly learn to respect you and your need for oxygen."

"Really?"

"That's exactly right."

"I never thought of that."

"Well, give it a try."

Then I told her that there were two other things she could—and definitely should—do to save her sanity while kissing these overly aggressive french kissers who made her gag. First, she should pull back and draw her mouth away from these boys, denying them the opportunity to french-kiss her like a vacuum cleaner. All she had to do was lean back and the kiss would be over, and she could breathe again. Second, she had a responsibility—to herself, most of all, but also to these obnoxious boys—to inform them verbally, in no uncertain terms, that they had to stop gagging her. "Just come right out and tell them that they're the ones making the mistake. 'I can't breathe with your tongue back there. Cut it out! Keep it in the front of my mouth, because if you don't you're going to be sorry.' And you can tell them that William Cane told you so."

This appreciative young woman leaned forward, eagerly thanking me.

After that experience I decided that in order to help these single women, I needed to provide a surrogate kisser. I had plenty of willing guys. I offered to pay these young men to kiss girls and teach them the self-confidence they needed. Over the next few months I hired and trained three male surrogates to teach women how to kiss. The number one technique these young women wanted to master was how to french kiss. My surrogates included an actor, a former student, and a politician. They were all handsome young men. I was always present for the lessons, directing the men in how to kiss the girls. After the first lesson that my politician surrogate gave, when the girl had departed, this young man turned to me and smiled.

"That was the most fun I ever had. Can you get me more of these lessons?"

Luke Marsh, one of my former students, became my primary male surrogate. Twenty-eight and very capable of making women feel at ease, he was familiar with every kiss in the book. Once when I couldn't be present, he even did a lesson alone, working from a prepared list of all the kisses in *The Art of Kissing.*

"Bill," he told me, "I didn't even need the list. The girl said she was interested in practicing the french kiss more than anything else. So we didn't get to the upside-down kiss, the vacuum kiss, or even the sliding kiss. It was a good lesson for her, she said, because I let her take control of the kisses and I gave her feedback. She made progress too. I assured her that if she ever needed a refresher she could come back for another lesson."

For many years I didn't have a female surrogate, even though plenty of single guys also wanted lessons. Primarily this was because the young women I had asked couldn't get permission from their boyfriends. But one day I was talking with my friend Gary Krasner, and I happened to mention that I was reading a terrific book, *The Conspiracy Against the Human Race*, a work of philosophy by Thomas Ligotti, the celebrated American horror writer. Gary said that his girlfriend, Celeste Aronson, had a PhD in philosophy and that I should talk with her about the book. Long story short, I called her and we chatted about Ligotti, Schopenhauer, Nietzsche, and current developments in neuroscience and consciousness, and shortly thereafter it occurred to me to ask this brilliant young woman whether she might be interested in working as a kissing surrogate. To my delight, she said yes, and she became my primary female surrogate. She also happened to be a dedicated weight lifter, and she was able to give terrific bear hugs to her students during lessons.

These private kissing lessons became so popular that I sometimes scheduled four on the same day. Before long the media picked up on these new developments, and magazines, newspapers, and television stations around the world began covering these so-called kissing classes. For some reason the Japanese media was particularly interested in the lessons. Probably this was because public kissing is so much rarer in Asia than in Europe and the United States, and this shyness about public displays of affection generated heightened interest in romantic affection.

The funny thing is that when we gave lessons to single men, Celeste and I often tried to engage them in conversations about Schopenhauer, Nietzsche, and Ligotti. It was disappointing to see how few young people were doing leisure reading. Most of our clients had never even heard of these philosophers, let alone read their books. And that's why I'm so glad you picked up this memoir about my college lecture circuit. As a reader, you and I are on the same wavelength. My idea to write *The Art of Kissing* literally spun my life into an entirely new direction, and if you've enjoyed hearing about the wonderful time I had directing hundreds of kissing shows then you too have been touched—hopefully in a positive way—by the powerful, I would even say unstoppable, romantic enthusiasm of American college students. I've lectured back and forth across the USA about kissing, and I still feel that my story is really *your* story—a wild joyride inspired by the vast multitudes of people who told me, over and over, how important they considered romantic kissing.